Refresher Course in GREGG SHORTHAND

Diamond Jubilee Series

Madeline S. Strony

Former Professor of Business Education
California State College
Los Angeles, California

M. Claudia Garvey

Former Member of Gregg Staff
Gregg Division
McGraw-Hill Book Company

Howard L. Newhouse

Vice President
Berkeley Schools
New York

Shorthand Written by *Charles Rader*

GREGG DIVISION
McGraw-Hill Book Company
New York St. Louis Dallas San Francisco Toronto London Sydney Mexico Panama

Book and cover design by Richard W. Stalzer.
Composition by H. D. Mann, Inc.
The text type—10/12 Univers, with Press Roman,
and special headings in Roman Compressed.

REFRESHER COURSE IN GREGG SHORTHAND, Diamond Jubilee Series

Library of Congress Catalog Card Number 74-98491

11 12 13 14 15   KPKP   8 3 2 1 0   ISBN 07-062205-1

ABOUT THIS BOOK

Have you taken a course in Gregg Shorthand in which you covered all the principles, yet because you've "been away from it" for a while, feel the need for a review? Then this book is for you. It is designed as a quick, yet thorough, review of Gregg Shorthand for those who have previously studied the system. If you have not had a complete course in Gregg, then this is *not* the book for you; you should study from a textbook that approaches the study of shorthand from the very beginning.

The purpose of this book is to review all the basic theory principles of the Gregg Shorthand system, to renew your knowledge of phrasing, to give you practice in writing shorthand that can be easily read (penmanship — fluency and proportion), and to "drive home" once and for all the brief forms that are so important in rapid writing.

THE BOOK IS ORGANIZED INTO 20 LESSONS

Lessons 1-15.　Each of these lessons contains the following parts:

1. *Know Your Alphabet.*　The better you know your alphabet, the more quickly you can construct outlines. This part of the lesson reviews for you the entire alphabet of Gregg Shorthand.

2. *Proportion Drill.*　Whether you write large or small shorthand notes is unimportant. It is very important, however, that the proportion of your shorthand characters be accurate, so that you can tell instantly whether you meant an *a* or an *e*, an *r* or an *l*, an *s, p* or *b,* and so on. The Proportion Drill will help you to write better shorthand—shorthand that is more easily transcribed.

3. *Principles.*　A complete review of the basic principles of Gregg Shorthand is provided in this part through the medium of carefully organized charts of words and phrases.

4. *Brief Forms and Phrases.*　This part of the lesson drills on the brief forms (all the brief forms in the Gregg system are presented), most-used phrases, and various special terms such as days of the week, months, and cities and states.

5. *Reading and Self-Dictation Practice.*　The Reading and Self-Dictation Practice consists of letters or articles in shorthand that emphasize the shorthand devices presented in the first four parts of the lesson. The plate content is tailored to the principles presented in each lesson, with a 90 percent or better coverage of each specific lesson. As many of the principles as possible are incorporated within the bounds of good letter writing. Employment of the principles is not, however, necessarily limited to those illustrated in the lesson charts. For example, *manufacture* is in the chart for Lesson 2; but *manufacturers* is used in one of the letters. In that way, you are reviewing two words instead of one. Your work with the shorthand in each Reading and Self-Dictation Practice will give you a further opportunity to speed up the relearning process; too, it will help you develop your shorthand writing speed.

The key to the Reading and Self-Dictation Practice exercises appears in the back of the book.

6. *Don't Let This Happen to You.* This special feature (appearing in Lessons 5, 10, 15, and 20) consists of examples of errors made by secretaries who misread their shorthand notes and failed to say what the dictator meant. Most of these errors came about because of poor proportion; others, because the stenographer did not use common sense in selecting the right word.

Lessons 16-20. These lessons provide a further review of the principles in Gregg Shorthand, but in a different form. Each lesson concentrates on a major principle of the system, as follows:

Lesson 16   Vowel Joinings
Lesson 17   Joined Word Beginnings
Lesson 18   Joined Word Endings
Lesson 19   Disjoined Word Beginnings and Endings
Lesson 20   Blends and the Omission of Vowels and Consonants

In each lesson you will find:

1. A review chart
2. A chart of 40 high-frequency words
3. A Reading and Self-Dictation Practice

INSIDE BACK COVER.   This chart includes all the brief forms listed alphabetically. The key is on page 122.

SUGGESTIONS FOR STUDY

Writing will always be easier if you READ aloud each section of the lesson first. Don't hesitate to use the key if you need it. You will probably use the key more frequently in the beginning lessons than you will in later ones.

Know Your Alphabet.   Read the outlines as quickly as you can. Read them through a second time. After reading, write the outlines once in the order in which they are given, saying them aloud as you write them. Write them a second time.

Proportion Drill.   Read the outline combinations and words before attempting to write them. Study the forms in order to see what is being emphasized in each drill—for example, *l* is about three times as large as *r; a* is huge, *e* is tiny. After reading and studying the Proportion Drill, make a shorthand copy of it. Compare your forms with those in the book; then copy the drill again.

Principles.   First read the brief explanation of the principles to be covered; then read the words across the columns, spelling any word you cannot immediately read. If after spelling you still cannot read a word, refer to the type key that appears below the drill. After reading the words across the columns, read down the columns. Try to check your reading time on each effort. When you have completed the readings, write each word twice, saying it aloud as you write.

Brief Forms, Phrases, and High-Frequency Words.   Read the outlines across the columns; then read down. Check with the key if necessary. Write each outline once, saying the word or phrase aloud as you write.

The brief-form chart at the back of the book can be used any time after Lesson 9. It is suggested that two minutes each day be spent in reading this chart: up, down, and across; sometimes starting with the first column; sometimes, with the last.

Reading and Self-Dictation Practice.   Always *read* the shorthand material (using the key if necessary) *before* writing it. If possible, check your reading time on your first effort; repeat the reading, again checking your time. Then dictate the material to yourself (think of this process as "self-dictation" rather than mere copying) in this way:

1. Silently read a convenient group of words (perhaps eight or ten) from the printed shorthand.

2. Then "dictate" that group to yourself aloud, writing each word or phrase as you say it.

Don't Let This Happen to You.   First, read what was dictated; then compare it with what was transcribed. You can readily see how the meaning can be changed by faulty proportion, lack of knowledge of the shorthand principles, or carelessness.

Concentrate on the principles of Gregg Shorthand and the development of good proportion in your notes during this part of your retraining program. If you do, you will find the next step—advanced dictation, speed development, and transcription—an easy transition.

Madeline S. Strony
M. Claudia Garvey
Howard L. Newhouse

LESSON 1

KNOW YOUR ALPHABET

k, g, r, l, n, m, t, d, h, th, a, e, i, o, u, s, f, v, s, p, b, sh, ch, j.

PROPORTION DRILL

Keep short strokes short, long strokes long. Make a's huge, e's tiny.

it-at, would, debt, eat, add, added, in-not, am, men, knee, me, many.

PRINCIPLES

Circle joinings.

1					
2					
3					
4					
5					
6					

1. easy, seen, grade, gave, take, meeting.
2. names, each, clearing, reader, agree, prepare.
3. attached, might, branch, chances, driver, paved.

4. seem, answer, chip, territory, three, tax.
5. skill, lake, telephone, tire, teams, bath.
6. James, lax, me, these, mail, history.

BRIEF FORMS AND PHRASES

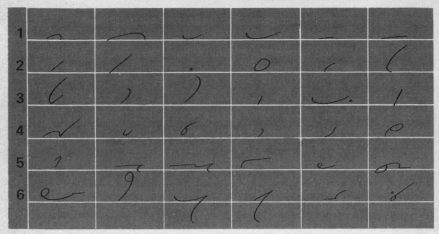

1. can, good, are-our-hour, will-well, in-not, am.
2. it-at, would, a-an, I, the, be-by.
3. but, for, have, shall, willing, which.
4. could, of, with, is-his, their-there, that.
5. wish, must, Mrs., them, year-were, I cannot.
6. I will not, I have, will be, to be, in the, he would.

READING AND SELF-DICTATION PRACTICE

1. Mr. Hale:

2. Dear Harry:

[Shorthand text - Gregg shorthand]

---

3. Dear Sir:

[Shorthand text - Gregg shorthand]

---

4. Dear Sir:

[Shorthand text - Gregg shorthand]

5. To Branch Managers:

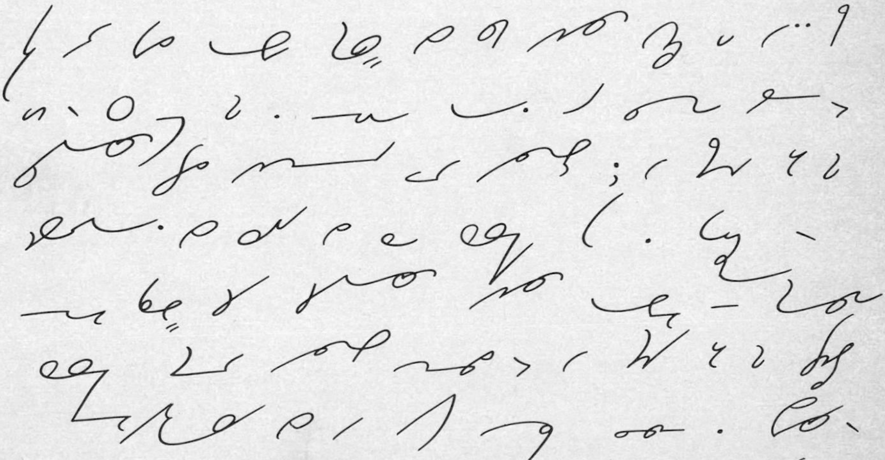

[shorthand text]

LESSON 2

s, f, v, s, p, b, ch, sh, j, t, d, ted, men, dif, ten, dem, ses, xes.

PROPORTION DRILL

Keep hooks deep and narrow.

of, are, will, you, can, good, you, this, the, ten, time, tomorrow.

PRINCIPLES

Hook vowels; <u>w</u> in the body of words; <u>ses</u>; word beginning <u>ex</u>; word endings
<u>sion-tion</u>, <u>tial</u>.

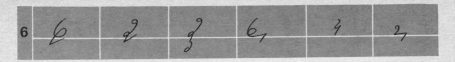

1. own, home, store, ball, whole, borrow.
2. drove, grown, cool, noon, do, move.
3. precious, cousin, plus, we, wait, waste.
4. queer, Broadway, driveway, quick, accessories, analysis.
5. sisters, express, explain, example, nation, action.
6. patient, efficient, efficiency, partial, social, essential.

BRIEF FORMS, SALUTATIONS, CLOSINGS, PHRASES, AND DAYS OF THE WEEK

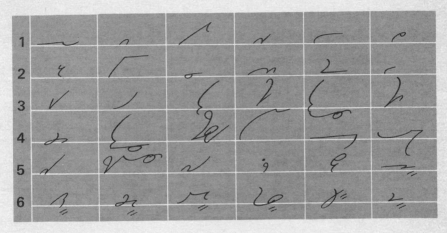

1. Mr., you-your, Dear Sir, Yours truly, them, they.
2. was, Dear Madam, when, Cordially yours, from, than.
3. should, and, business, Yours very truly, businesslike, Very truly yours.
4. Sincerely yours, businessman, advertised, Dear Mr., manufacture, will not be.
5. your order, I should like, you want, he is, I was, Monday.
6. Tuesday, Wednesday, Thursday, Friday, Saturday, Sunday.

READING AND SELF-DICTATION PRACTICE

6. Dear Madam:

[Shorthand text]

226

2:30

---

7. Dear Mr. Wade:

[Shorthand text]

---

8. Dear Mr. Wooley:

[Shorthand text]

50

75

9. Dear Mrs. Quimby:

125

[shorthand]

---

10. Dear Cousin Carol: *[shorthand]*

[shorthand]

---

11. Dear Sir: *[shorthand]*

[shorthand]

LESSON 3

KNOW YOUR ALPHABET

Notice the combination of strokes.

k, r, kr, l, g, lg, kl, gr, gl, rk.

PROPORTION DRILL

Give r and l an upward turn at the finish for rd and ld. Write the nt-nd, mt-md blends upward from the line of writing.

fear, feared, fill, filled, sent, seemed, hear, heard, hint, own, owned, old, foamed.

PRINCIPLES

Amounts; word beginnings be, de, re, dis, mis; word endings ly, ily, ally; rd, ld.

1					
2					
3					
4					
5					
6					

1. 300, 3,000, 300,000, $3, $300, 3 bushels.
2. $300,000, 3 cents, $3.25, 3 percent, few hundred, 3 million.
3. 3 pounds, became, delaying, describe, mistake, research.
4. deposit, repaired, heard, ignored, child, children.
5. cold, older, early, only, readily, family.
6. likely, totally, socially, retail, decrease, retire.

BRIEF FORMS, PHRASES, AND MONTHS

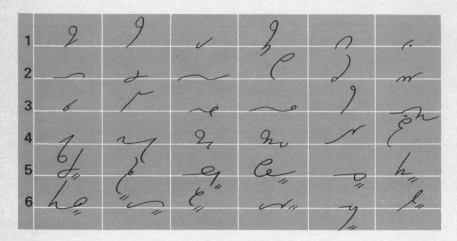

1. after, advantage, what, advantageous, this, thing-think.
2. enclose, send, glad, about, very, worth.
3. yet, during, correspond-correspondence, gladly, ever-every, enclosure.
4. to be able, you will be, as soon as, as you know, into the, has been.
5. January, February, March, April, May, June.
6. July, August, September, October, November, December.

READING AND SELF-DICTATION PRACTICE

12. Dear Mr. Field:

[shorthand]

---

13. Dear Mr. Arnold: [shorthand]

[shorthand]

642-4121 [shorthand]

---

14. Dear Mr. Ramos: [shorthand]

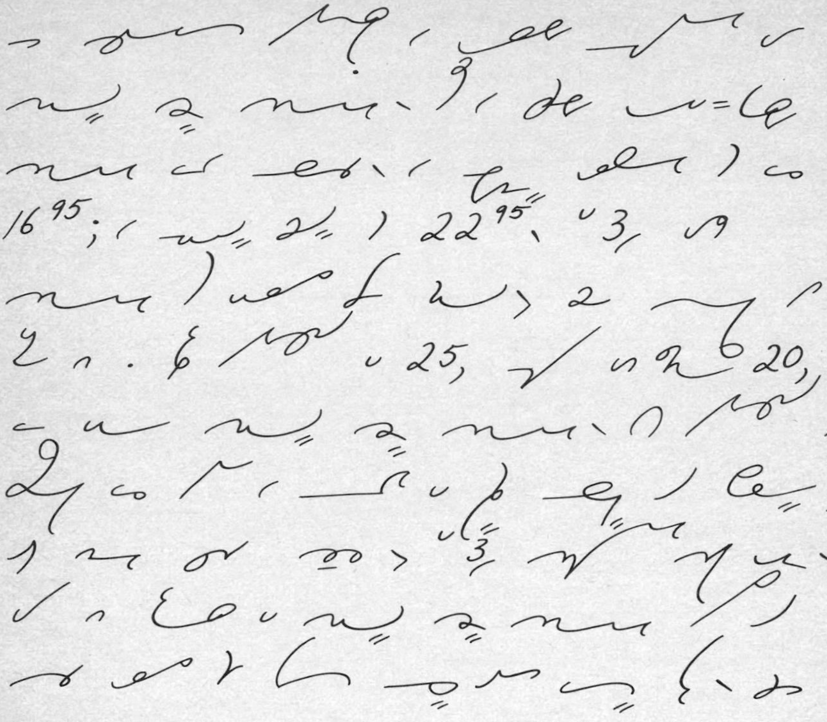

15. Dear Subscriber: 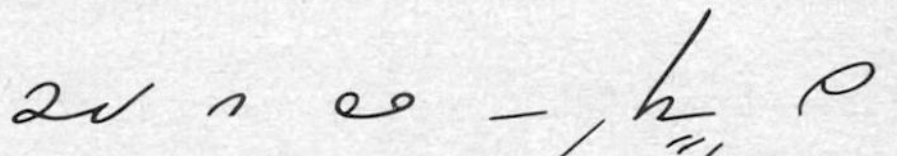

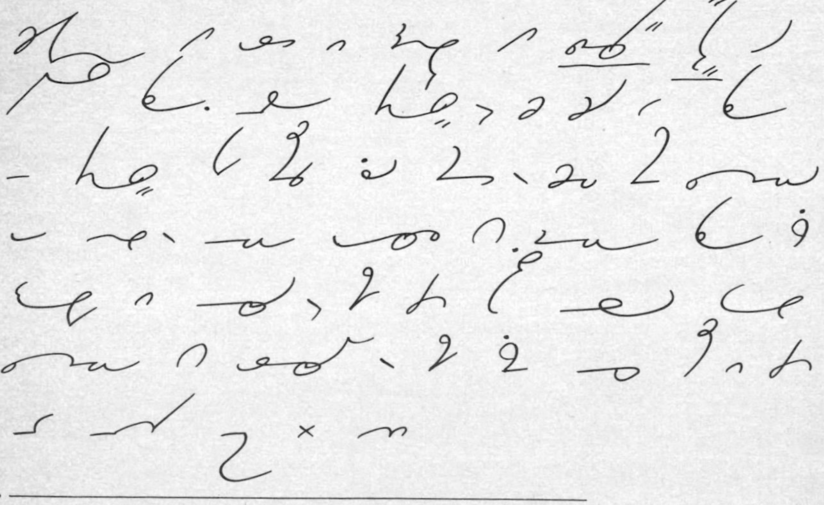

16. Dear Mr. Kenmore: 

LESSON 4

KNOW YOUR ALPHABET

st, ts, ds, sn, ns, sns, sts, sm, sms, sd, sds.

PROPORTION DRILL

N and m are horizontal; ng and nk slant downward. Note that nk is longer than ng.

ban, bang, bank, brain, blame, blank, in, am, ink, seen, sing, sink.

PRINCIPLES

Word endings ure, ture; ual, tual; ng, nk; y, ye, ya; aw, ah.

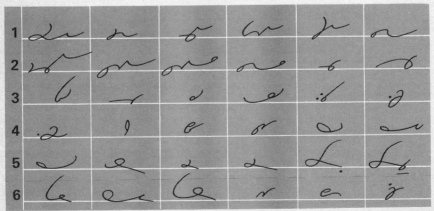

1. failure, secure, nature, picture, feature, equal.
2. schedule, actual, actually, equally, neither, gather.
3. bother, mother, either, leather, ahead, away.
4. aware, yes, yacht, youth, yard, yellow.

5. yield, rank, sing, sink, banking, banquet.
6. bring, along, blank, other, yoke, whether.

BRIEF FORMS, PHRASES, CITIES, AND STATES

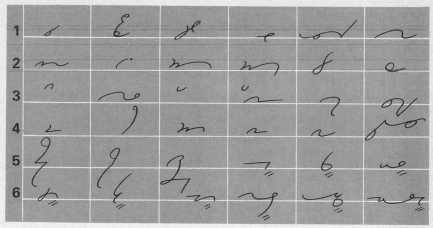

1. yet, experience, satisfy-satisfactory, next, regard, great.
2. worker, thank, suggest, suggestion, particular, where.
3. under, greatly, over, overcome, company, accompanied.
4. soon, ever-every, success, one-won, you are, I would like.
5. I have not been, I shall be, thank you very much, Michigan, Pennsylvania, Oregon.
6. Chicago, Boston, New York, Cleveland, Los Angeles, New Orleans.

READING AND SELF-DICTATION PRACTICE

17. Dear Mr. Franklin:

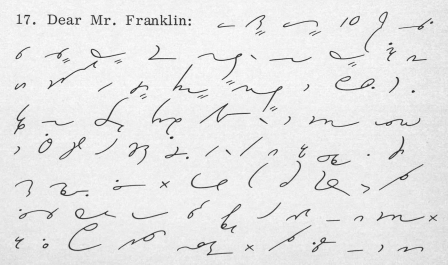

[Shorthand text continues from previous page]

---

18. Dear Mrs. Jackson: *[shorthand]*

[shorthand lines]

---

19. Dear Mr. Singer: *[shorthand]*

[shorthand lines]

(shorthand)

---

20. Dear Mr. Lopez: *(shorthand)*

---

21. Dear Mr. Didham: *(shorthand)*

LESSON 5

KNOW YOUR ALPHABET

s, f, v, s, p, b, sh, ch, j, a, e, i, o, oo.

PROPORTION DRILL

<u>S</u> is a small curve; <u>oo</u> is a deep hook; <u>sh</u>, <u>ch</u>, and <u>j</u> are straight downstrokes.

see, say, we, way, several, we have, she is, chief, session, we shall, sage, wage.

PRINCIPLES

Blends <u>ten-den-tain</u>, <u>tem-dem</u>; omission of short <u>u</u>; omission of minor vowels; word endings <u>ment</u>, <u>able-ible</u>.

1. acceptance, bulletin, extension, straighten, danger, audience.
2. evidence, guidance, ascertain, certainly, obtain, attempt.
3. estimate, automatic, customer, system, damage, freedom.
4. seldom, random, summer, funny, judge, brush.
5. come, done, courteous, serious, genuine, theory.
6. shipment, payment, treatment, terrible, possible, available.

BRIEF FORMS AND PHRASES

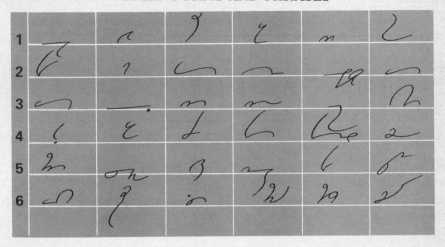

1. important-importance, those, several, opinion, world, value.
2. between, wish, progress, gone, merchandise, organize.
3. organization, morning, work, worker, envelope, difficult.
4. putting, opportunity, general, big, bigness, we will.
5. if you can, I am sure, thank you for, you must have, by the, I do not.
6. on this, we shall be, he can, if you want, if that is, we wanted.

READING AND SELF-DICTATION PRACTICE

22. Dear Mr. Weeks:

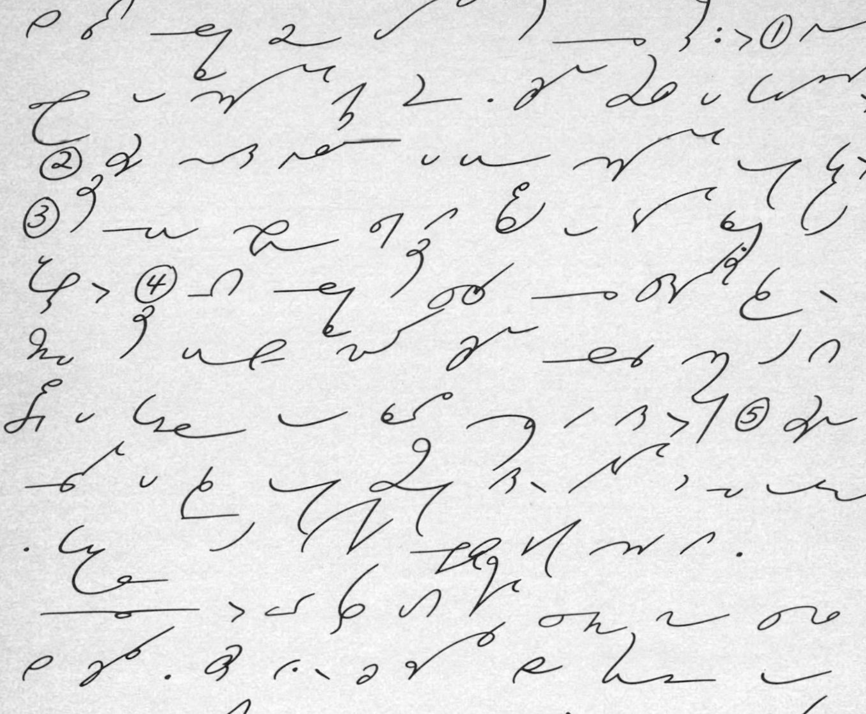

23. Dear Mrs. Swift:

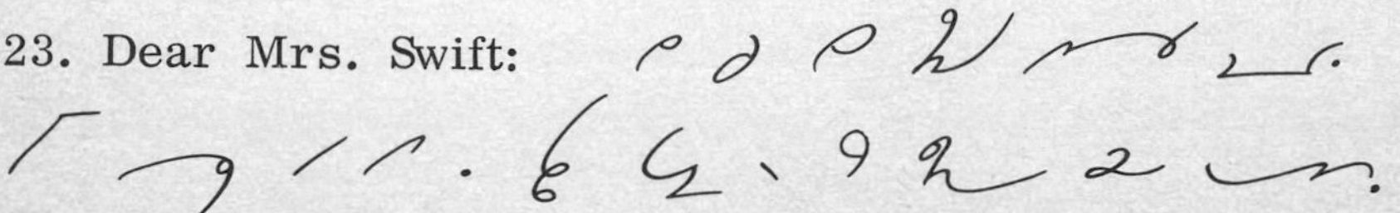

PTA ... 10 ...

7:30 ... "2 ..."

413-1612 ... 21 ...

---

24. Dear Mrs. Lane:

PTA ... 10 ... 26

10 ...

[Shorthand notes]

---

25. To the Staff:

[Shorthand notes]

2651 - jh *[shorthand]*

---

26. Dear Mr. Jones:

[Shorthand notes]

DON'T LET THIS HAPPEN TO YOU!

DICTATED	TRANSCRIBED

1. This can be finished in an hour.

1. You can be finished in an hour.

2. He will not bother you with the details.

2. He will not bore you with the details.

3. Did you each make a contribution?

3. Did you ever make a contribution?

4. Your success was easy to understand, as you had worked hard.

4. Your suggestion was easy to understand, as you had worked hard.

5. The film was one we had not seen before.

5. The firm was one we had not seen before.

LESSON 6

[shorthand characters]

a, e, i, ī̄a, ĭa, o, oo, u, ow, oi.

PROPORTION DRILL

[shorthand characters]

known, noon, core, coal, cool, bone, boon, shows, shoes, chose, choose, shore, sure, oil, real.

PRINCIPLES

The sounds of <u>oi</u>, <u>ū</u>, <u>ow</u>; blends <u>ted-ded-det</u>, <u>men-mem</u>, <u>nt-nd</u>, <u>mt-md</u>.

1	*[shorthand]*	*[shorthand]*	*[shorthand]*	*[shorthand]*	*[shorthand]*
2	*[shorthand]*	*[shorthand]*	*[shorthand]*	*[shorthand]*	*[shorthand]*
3	*[shorthand]*	*[shorthand]*	*[shorthand]*	*[shorthand]*	*[shorthand]*
4	*[shorthand]*	*[shorthand]*	*[shorthand]*	*[shorthand]*	*[shorthand]*
5	*[shorthand]*	*[shorthand]*	*[shorthand]*	*[shorthand]*	*[shorthand]*
6	*[shorthand]*	*[shorthand]*	*[shorthand]*	*[shorthand]*	*[shorthand]*

1. Roy, soil, annoyance, now, proud, doubt.
2. unite, review, unit, treated, study, today.
3. detail, mention, month, minute, memory, memo.
4. retain, tenant, signed, explained, kind, event.
5. into, entire, prevent, windows, print, sent.
6. empty, prompt, blamed, exempt, trimmed, claimed.

BRIEF FORMS, PHRASES, CITIES, AND STATES

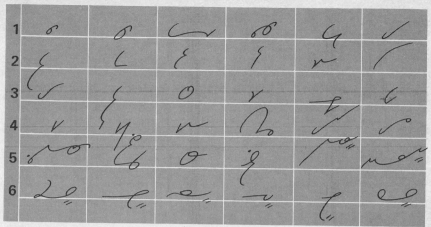

1. use, out-how, progressed, without, purpose, order.
2. public, upon, speak, such, street, time.
3. ordinary, publish-publication, why, state, merchant, part.
4. short, shortage, shorter, difficulty, ordered, ordinarily.
5. he would like, has been made, why not, there has been, Detroit, Toledo.
6. Philadelphia, Minneapolis, California, Missouri, Nebraska, Alabama.

READING AND SELF-DICTATION PRACTICE

27. Dear Mr. Royal:

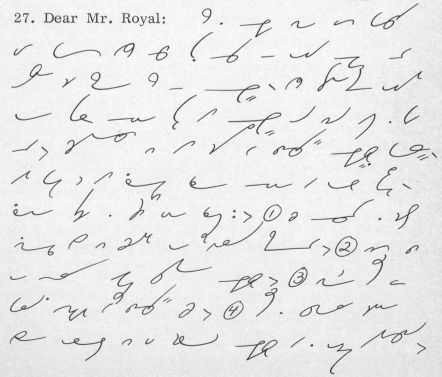

[Shorthand text]

---

28. Dear Roy:

[Shorthand text]

29. Dear Mr. Vargas:

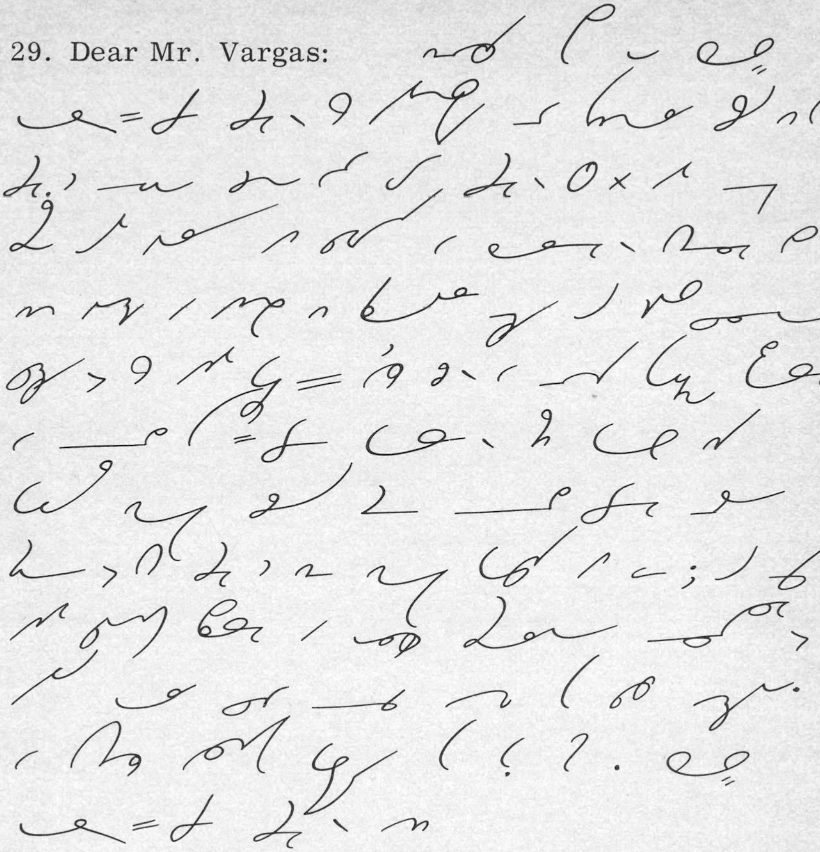

[shorthand content]

---

30. Ralph Shorter:

[shorthand content]

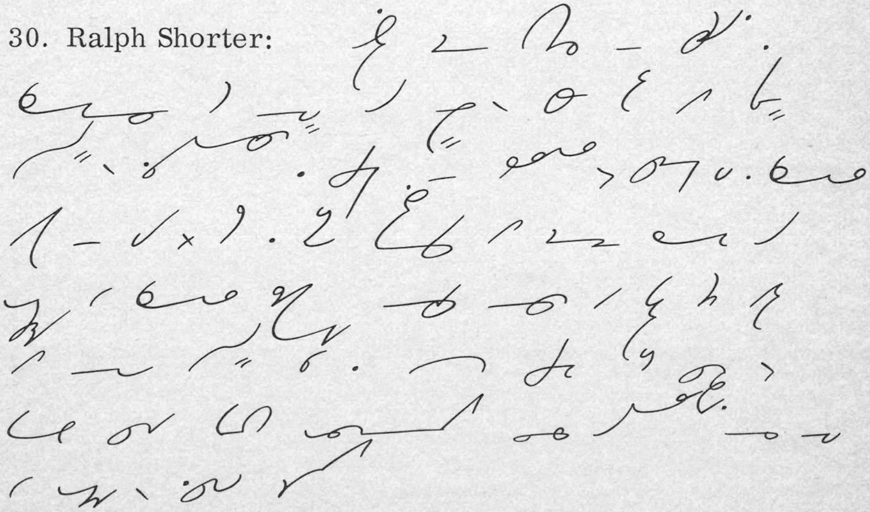

LESSON 7

KNOW YOUR ALPHABET

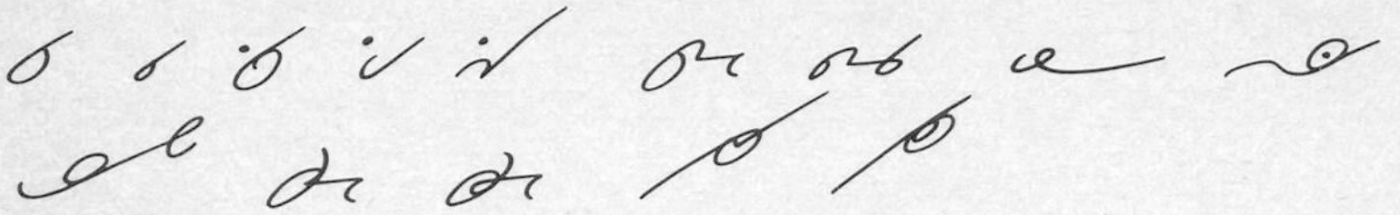

ate, eat, height, hot, hood, ounce, unit, oil, create, radio, signs, science, died, diet.

PROPORTION DRILL

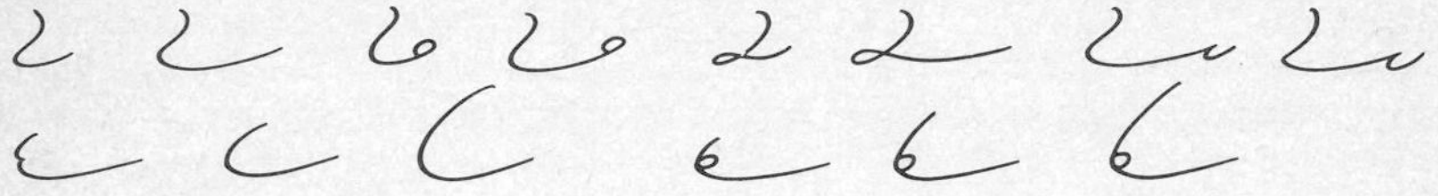

fr, fl, free, flee, fear, feel, flow, furlough, sl, pl, bl, sell, peel, bell.

PRINCIPLES

Vowel combinations īa, ēa, ĭo; omission of vowel in ition-ation when preceded by t, d, n, m; omission of r in the combinations tern-dern, term-derm, thern-therm, ort; word beginnings per, pur.

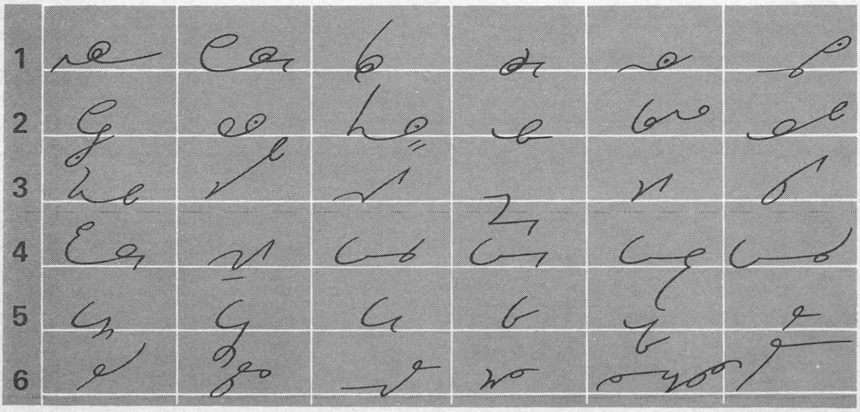

1. trial, appliance, bias, science, create, media.
2. appreciate, area, Julia, rayon, poetry, radio.
3. folio, studio, condition, information, station, addition.
4. explanation, quotation, permit, permission, permissible, permanent.
5. pursue, purchase, purse, port, report, turn.
6. turned, attorney, modern, southern, thermostatic, determine.

BRIEF FORMS AND COMPOUNDS

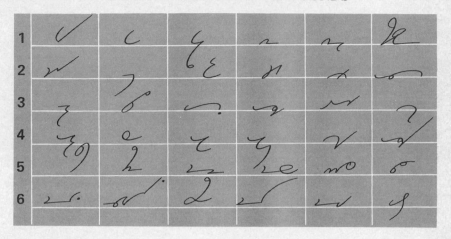

1. parted, present, probably, one-won, once-ones, advertisement.
2. stated, never, speaker, situation, quantity, regular.
3. newspaper, idea, organizing, request, throughout, company.
4. responsible, where, represent, representative, questioned, requested.
5. however, everyone, someone, somewhere, worthwhile, within.
6. something, notwithstanding, everywhere, sometime, somewhat, whatever.

READING AND SELF-DICTATION PRACTICE

31. Dear Mr. Bryan:

[Shorthand content — not transcribable as text]

32. To the Staff:

[Shorthand content — not transcribable as text] 613,

33. Dear Miss Porter:

[Shorthand content — not transcribable as text]

[Shorthand text]

---

34. Dear Mr. Brierly: [Shorthand text continues]

[Shorthand includes the notations 21 and 1260]

(shorthand)

---

35. Dear Mr. Turner: *(shorthand)*

(shorthand)

---

36. Dear Mr. Sanchez: *(shorthand)*

(shorthand)

LESSON 8

KNOW YOUR ALPHABET

[shorthand characters]

kg, kr, kl, kn, km, kt, kd, kf, kv, kash, kach, kaj, she, sher, cher, jal.

PROPORTION DRILL

[shorthand characters]

hunt, who would, day, today, aid, aided, one, come, whom, common, some, summon, summer, former.

PRINCIPLES

Word endings ings, ingly; word beginnings con, com, en, in, un, em, im, for, fore, fur.

1					
2					
3					
4					
5					

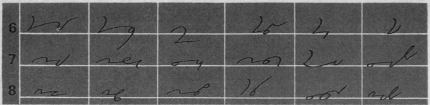

1. feelings, doings, comings, knowingly, exceedingly, concerning.
2. confidence, confident, confirm, confer, concluded, compete.
3. complete, compose, enrich, encouragement, increase, income.
4. indeed, insist, invest, unfair, unfinished, embarrass.
5. emphasis, employ, employee, impossible, import, impatient.
6. forgotten, forgive, conform, furniture, furnish, further.
7. connote, commerce, emotion, connection, furlough, immodest.
8. unknown, uneasy, committee, forehead, enact, unnoticed.

BRIEF FORMS, PHRASES, CITIES, AND STATES

1. immediate, immediately, valuable, opinions, opinionated, object.
2. objection, particulars, subject, subjects, successful, successfully.
3. disadvantage, advantageous, acknowledge, acknowledged, acknowledgment, recognize.
4. they might be, to this, hear from you, it will be, I will be able, if we are.
5. we shall have, Los Angeles, Kansas City, New York, Pittsburgh, Portland.
6. Washington, Virginia, Vermont, New Mexico, South Dakota, Houston.

READING AND SELF-DICTATION PRACTICE

37. Dear Mrs. Washington:

38. To Plant Managers in Houston, Los Angeles, and Portland:

39. Dear Jack:

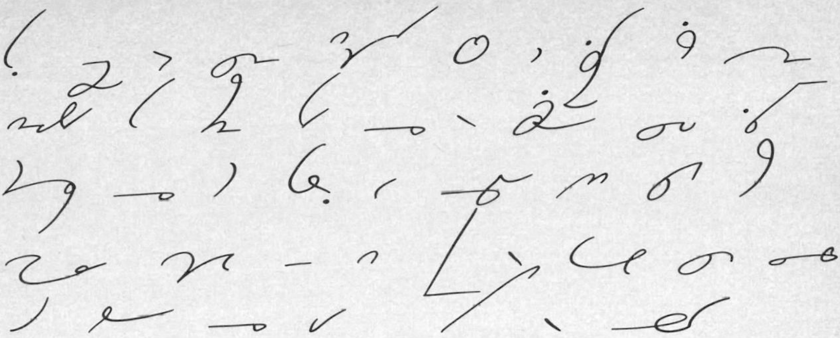

[shorthand text]

---

40. Dear Mr. Conover: [shorthand text]

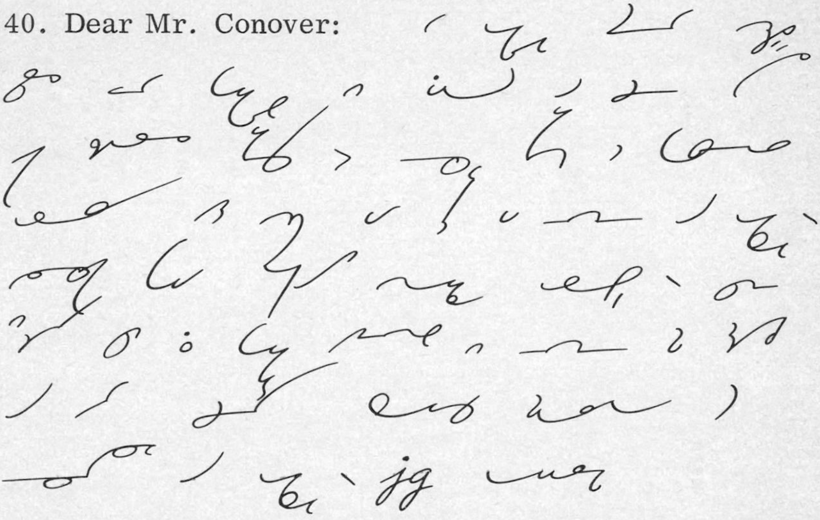

41. Antonio Rafael: [shorthand text]

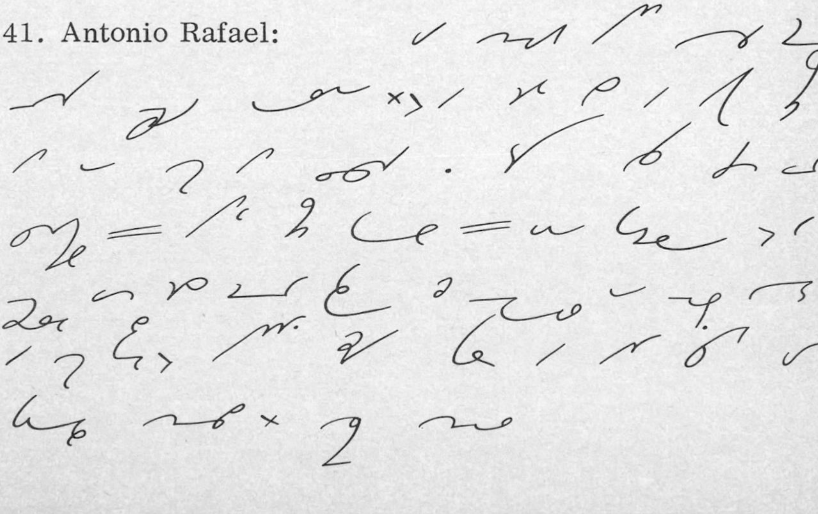

LESSON 9

KNOW YOUR ALPHABET

oo, k, gay, th, ten, tem, o, r, th, nd, md, r, rd, l, ld.

PROPORTION DRILL

writ, rate, rather, rated, reach, ridge, ledge, large, rave, laugh, leaf, live.

PRINCIPLES

Business phrases; def-div, dev, div.

1. of course, as soon as, as soon as possible, of this, I am sure, to us.
2. let us, let us know, to do, to know, to me, to make.
3. into this, I hope, I hope you will, we hope, your order, thank you for your order.
4. days ago, years ago, I want, you want, he wants, one of the.
5. will you please, up to date, definite, defeat, define, differ.
6. different, difference, devote, develop, divide, dividend.

BRIEF FORMS AND DERIVATIVES

1. yesterday, recognized, railroad, govern, government, governor.
2. otherwise, character, characterize, satisfied, understand, understood.
3. judgment, greater, greatest, worked, worker, businesses.
4. businessmen, suggested, suggestion, suggestive, particularly, questions.
5. unquestionable, progressed, progressive, progressively, manufactured, manufacturer.
6. parts, depart, department, wishing, wishes, wishful.

READING AND SELF-DICTATION PRACTICE

42. To All Department Heads:

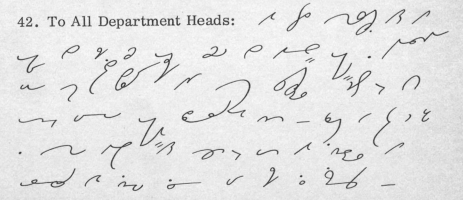

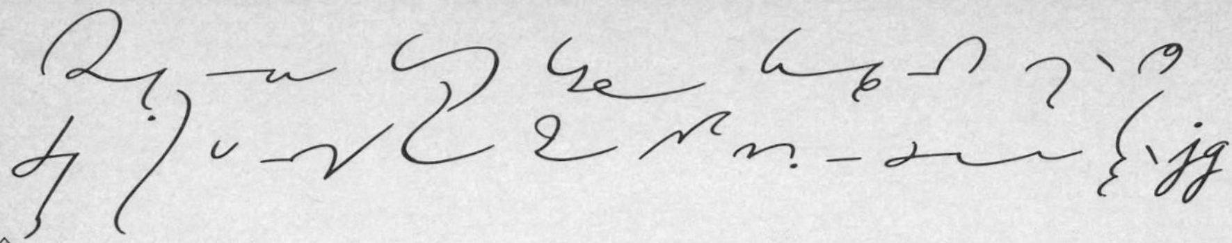

[Shorthand text]

---

43. Dear Mr. Defferman: [Shorthand text]

[Shorthand text]

44. Dear Mr. Devlin: [Shorthand text]

[Shorthand text]

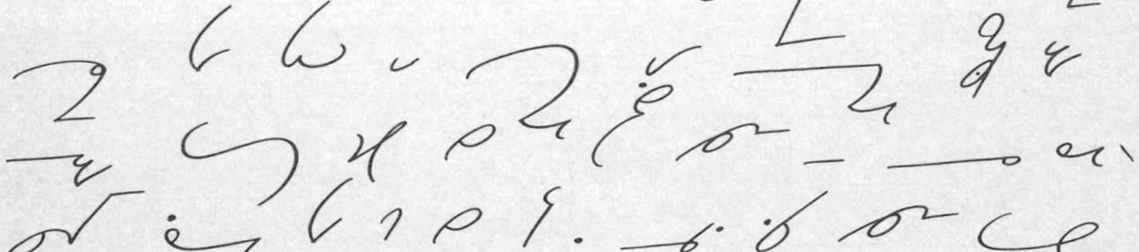

45. Dear Mr. Campo:

46. Martin Baxter:

LESSON 10

KNOW YOUR ALPHABET

fr, fer, fel, fk, fek, fag, pr, per, pel, vg, vag, vl, val, bl, bel.

PROPORTION DRILL

the, they, that, than, you, this, you, can, good, were, either, end, where, aired, ail, ailed.

PRINCIPLES

Word beginnings al, ul, (syllable ul), sub, electr-electric; word endings cle-cal, self, selves; intersection.

1. almost, already, also, altogether, ultimate, result.
2. consult, adult, subscribe, submit, substance, electric.
3. electrical, electricity, electric iron, electric wire, electrolysis, electrocuted.
4. article, chronicle, practical, medical, critical, political.
5. herself, yourself, itself, oneself, myself, themselves.
6. ourselves, a.m., p.m., chamber of commerce, c.o.d., Great Britain.

BRIEF FORMS AND PHRASES

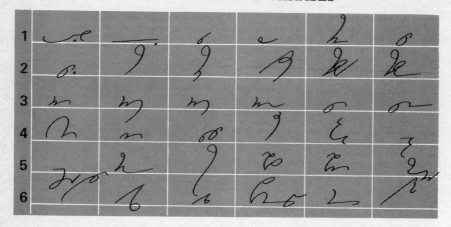

1. willingness, morning, yet, were, everyone, how-out.
2. outing, advantage, advantageous, disadvantage, advertised, advertisement.
3. success, successive, successful, successor, acknowledge, acknowledgment.
4. difficult, work, without, several, speakers, newspaper.
5. in fact, if you will, I have been, we hope that, we hope you can, as a result.
6. to make, would be able, to see, about this matter, from you, to do so.

READING AND SELF-DICTATION PRACTICE

47. Gentlemen:

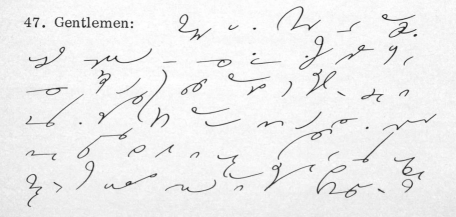

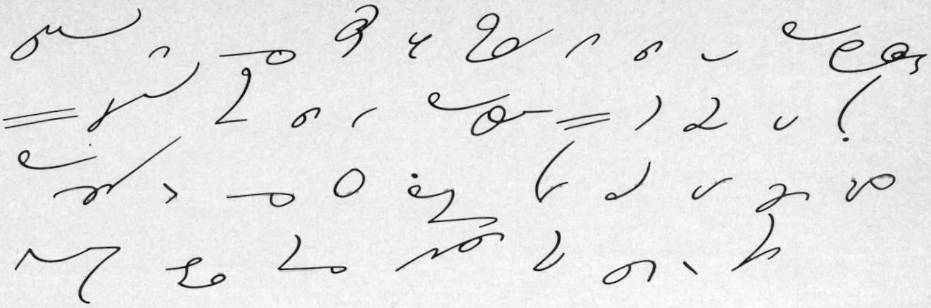

48. Dear John:

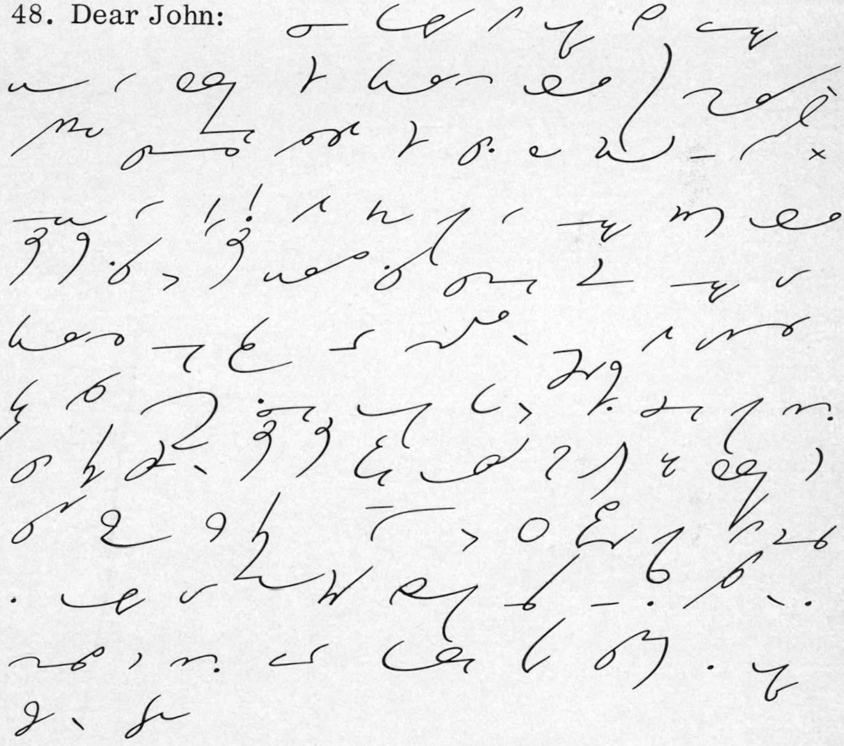

49. Gentlemen:

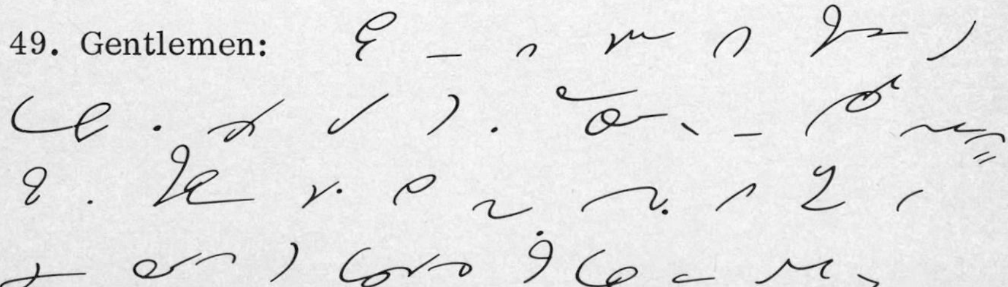

50. Dear Mr. Chipley:

51. Dear Doctor Garcia:

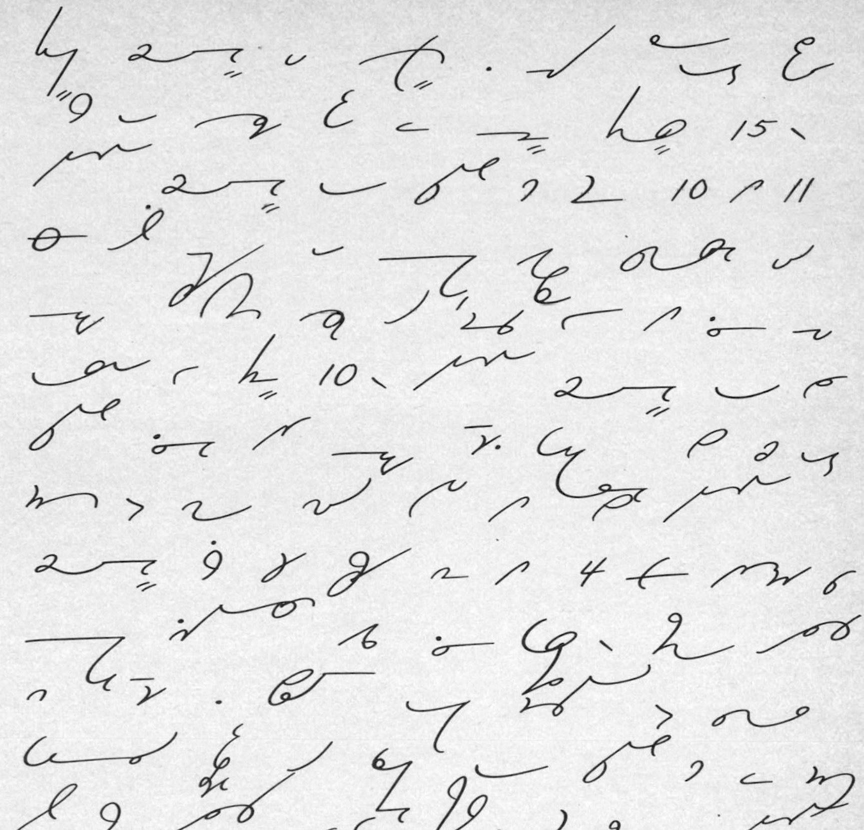

DON'T LET THIS HAPPEN TO YOU!

DICTATED	TRANSCRIBED
(shorthand 1)	*(shorthand 1)*
(shorthand 2)	*(shorthand 2)*
(shorthand 3)	*(shorthand 3)*
(shorthand 4)	*(shorthand 4)*
(shorthand 5)	*(shorthand 5)*

DICTATED

1. As you are aware of the situation, you may come with us.

2. The desk was so badly chipped we could not accept it.

3. The color was unsuitable.

4. The cage was too small to hold the pets.

5. We would like to catch the first edition if possible.

TRANSCRIBED

1. If you are aware of the situation, you may come with us.

2. The desk was so badly shipped we could not accept it.

3. The collar was unsuitable.

4. The cave was too small to hold the pets.

5. We would like to cash the first edition if possible.

LESSON 11

KNOW YOUR ALPHABET

n, m, ng, nk, s, p, b, s, f, v, r, rd, nt, l, ld, mt.

PROPORTION DRILL

as, half, if, advantage, asked, affect, effect, yesterday, effort, after, afford, avid.

PRINCIPLES

Word beginnings inter-enter-intro, post, super, trans; word endings ship, ful, ification.

51

1. interfere, interior, internal, interpret, interpretation, interrupt.
2. interview, enter, entered, entering, enterprising, entrance.
3. introduce, introduction, postmark, postpaid, postpone, post office.
4. superb, superior, supervised, supervisor, transact, transaction.
5. transfer, transferred, transmit, transmission, ownership, township.
6. relationships, membership, helpful, successful, modification, specification.

FREQUENTLY USED WORDS

Below are 40 of the most frequently used words. (You will notice that you have learned many of them as brief forms.)

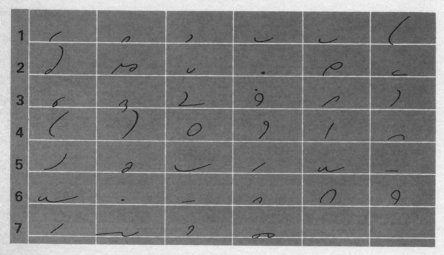

1. the, you, is, are, our, by.
2. very, truly, of, a, that, on.
3. with, yours, from, has, to, for.
4. be, have, I, if, which, can.
5. and, we, will, it, or, not.
6. all, an, in, your, this, as.
7. at, Mr., us, any.

READING AND SELF-DICTATION PRACTICE

52. Dear Mr. Harrold:

53. Dear Mr. Paragon:

54. Dear Friend:

55. John Quincy:

LESSON 12

KNOW YOUR ALPHABET

s, sh, ch, j, po, pr, pl, bo, br, bl.

PROPORTION DRILL

soon, some, from, knee, me, many, cannot, come, common, it, would, debt.

PRINCIPLES

Word endings ther, gram, rity, lity-lty, hood-ward; syllables thern, therm; phrases.

1. neither, rather, other, together, southern, northern.
2. thermometer, thermos, of course, let us know, we shall be glad, two or three.
3. to make, we hope you will, has been, it has been, as soon as, as soon as possible.

4. telegram, program, authority, majority, minority, ability.
5. responsibility, personality, punctuality, faculty, locality, qualities.
6. loyalty, afterward, forward, backward, neighborhood, boyhood.

FREQUENTLY USED WORDS

Here are 40 additional words of high frequency.

1. would, one, please, now, more, should.
2. who, about, dear, been, they, year.
3. no, gentlemen, sincerely, know, order, these.
4. so, there, letter, service, make, enclosed.
5. time, may, new, business, their, some.
6. out, were, was, do, but, office.
7. other, them, than, information.

READING AND SELF-DICTATION PRACTICE

56. Dear Fred:

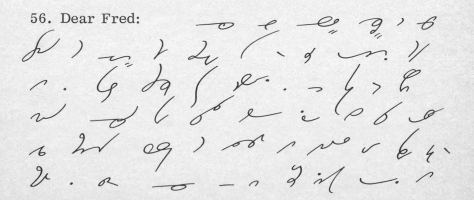

(shorthand content)

---

57. Dear Mr. Gomez: *(shorthand content)*

(shorthand content)
16 *(shorthand content)*
(shorthand content)
(shorthand content)
(shorthand content)
(shorthand content) 26 *(shorthand content)*
(shorthand content)
(shorthand content)
(shorthand content)
(shorthand content)

58. Gentlemen: *[shorthand]*

---

59. Dear Mr. North: *[shorthand]*

---

60. Dear Mr. Sothern: *[shorthand]*

61. Gentlemen:

25

48

LESSON 13

n, m, men, th, nt, mt, th, ten, tem, oo, k, gay, dev, o, r, rd, l, ld.

PROPORTION DRILL

you, use, he can, I, how, I can, own, home, whole, core, call, goal, gold, gaunt.

PRINCIPLES

Word beginnings, self-circum, under; word endings sume, sumption, ulate, ulation; proper name terminations.

1. selfish, self-made, self-control, self-satisfied, circumstance, circumstances.
2. circumstantial, understand, misunderstand, understood, misunderstood, undergo.
3. assume, resume, presume, consumer, assumption, consumption.
4. resumption, regulate, speculate, circulate, tabulation, accumulation.
5. Harrisburg, Pittsburgh, Nashville, Jacksonville, Springfield, Stamford.
6. Washington, Lexington, Birmingham, Johnston, Johnstown, Evanston.

FREQUENTLY USED WORDS

Here are 40 more words of high frequency.

1. up, made, he, just, my, such.
2. his, help, each, sales, department, am.
3. had, use, program, every, me, also.
4. send, work, price, first, amount, want.
5. when, manager, two, get, like, its.
6. under, much, only, many, good, what.
7. copy, most, find, how.

62. Dear Mr. Johnston: *[shorthand]*

[shorthand lines]

---

63. Dear Mrs. Oxford: *[shorthand]*

64. Dear Mr. Perry:

[Shorthand text]

---

65. Dear Mr. Grant: *[Shorthand text]*

LESSON 14

KNOW YOUR ALPHABET

k, g, r, l, n, m, ka, ga, ak, ag, ra, la, ar, al, ne, ma, an, em.

PROPORTION DRILL

keys, guess, case, gaze, rest, least, next, miss, teas, days, fees, face.

PRINCIPLES

Abbreviations—word families: <u>titude</u>, <u>titute</u>, <u>quire</u>, <u>ntic</u>, <u>ology</u>, <u>tribute</u>, <u>quent</u>, <u>itis</u>, <u>iety</u>.

1. aptitude, gratitude, substitute, substitution, institute, institution.
2. constitute, constitution, inquire, inquires, inquired, inquiry.
3. requirements, frantic, authentic, Atlantic, apology, apologize.
4. psychology, psychologist, psychological, attribute, contribute, contributed.
5. contribution, distribute, distribution, distributor, frequent, frequently.
6. subsequent, consequently, tonsillitis, neuritis, society, propriety.

FREQUENTLY USED WORDS

Here are 40 additional words of high frequency.

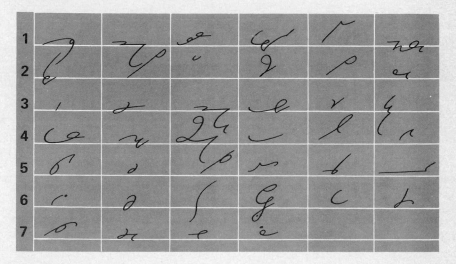

1. give, number, return, president, during, insurance.
2. best, today, over, after, day, years.
3. shall, same, numbers, last, state, possible.
4. plan, cost, available, well, days, those.
5. attention, see, date, through, need, month.
6. thank, way, before, appreciate, per, check.
7. take, since, next, here.

READING AND SELF-DICTATION PRACTICE

66. Mr. Rivera:

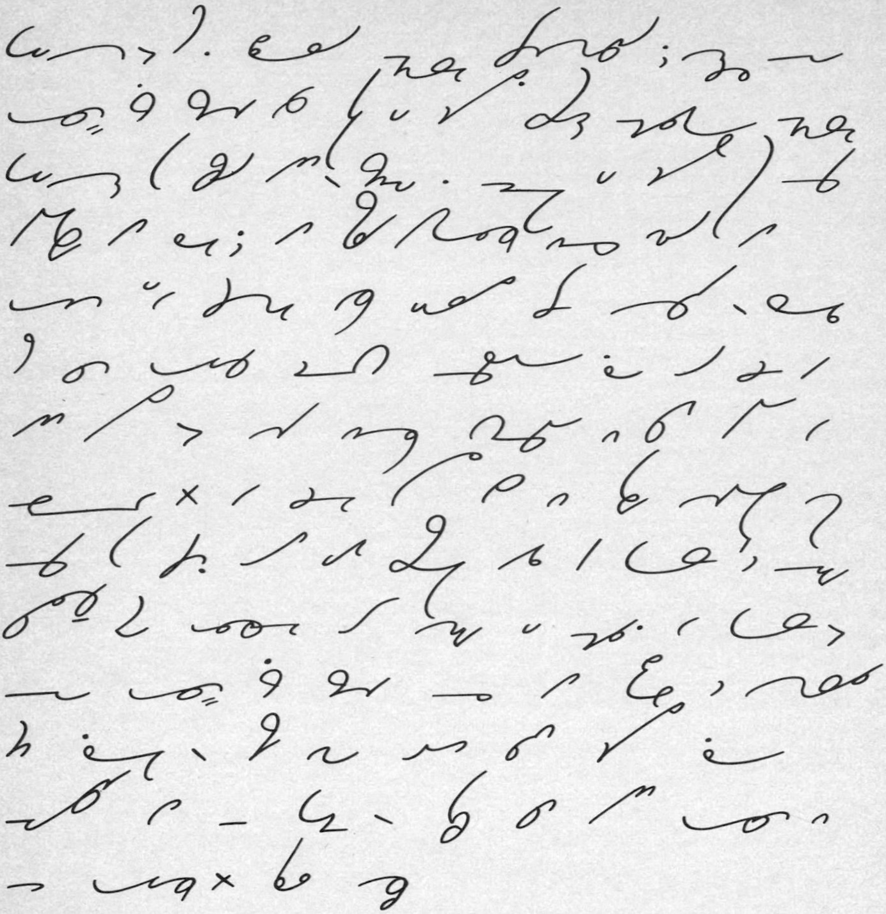

67. Dear Mrs. Nestor:

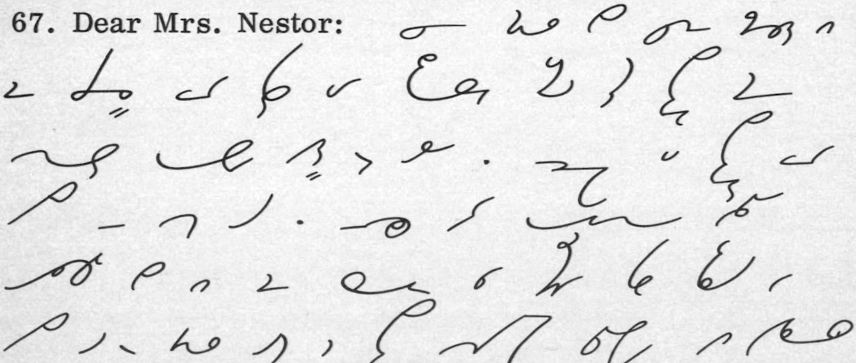

[Shorthand notation]

---

68. Dear Doctor Fisher: *[Shorthand notation]*

[Shorthand notation]

---

69. Dear Mrs. Conant: *[Shorthand notation]*

[Shorthand notation]

[Gregg shorthand outline]

---

70. Dear Dean Edens: *[Gregg shorthand outline]*

---

71. Dear Miss Brady: *[Gregg shorthand outline]*

LESSON 15

sks, sgs, sns, sms, sts, sds, sth, stn, stm.

PROPORTION DRILL

seek, sake, sag, sheer, cheer, jeer, here, heard, held, those, tense, tennis, temper, temple.

PRINCIPLES

Abbreviations—not in families; omission of words in phrases; common geographical abbreviations.

1. privilege, anniversary, significant-significance, arithmetic, convenient-convenience, inconvenient-inconvenience.
2. alphabetic, memorandum, equivalent, reluctant-reluctance, by the way, at a time.
3. one or two, in addition to the, some of these, in the past, out of the, up to date.

4. out of town, some of our, some of them, will you please, week or two, one of our.
5. America, American, England, English, Great Britain, Honolulu.
6. Puerto Rico, Canada, U.S., U.S.A., Hawaii, Pacific.

FREQUENTLY USED WORDS

Here are 40 additional words of high frequency.

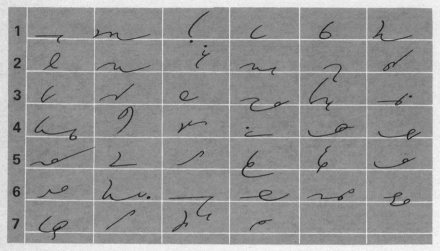

1. must, school, being, present, pay, full.
2. tax, call, hope, course, company, used.
3. part, could, where, complete, because, meeting.
4. policy, however, stock, home, line, list.
5. credit, form, into, people, special, let.
6. three, following, members, mail, committee, necessary.
7. prices, do, few, then.

READING AND SELF-DICTATION PRACTICE

72. Dear Mrs. Held:

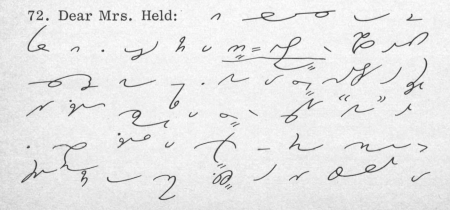

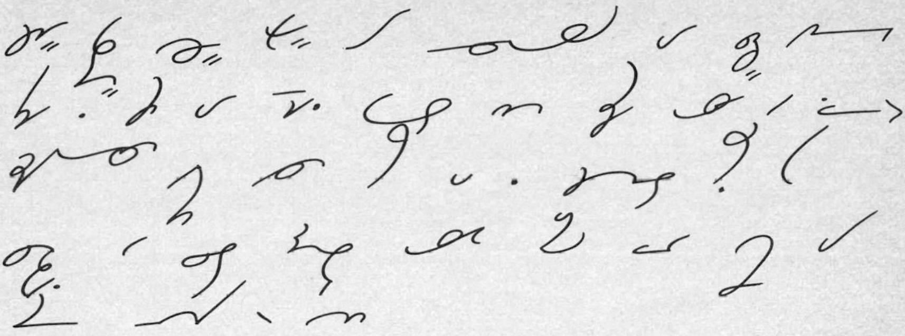

73. Memo to Executive Personnel:

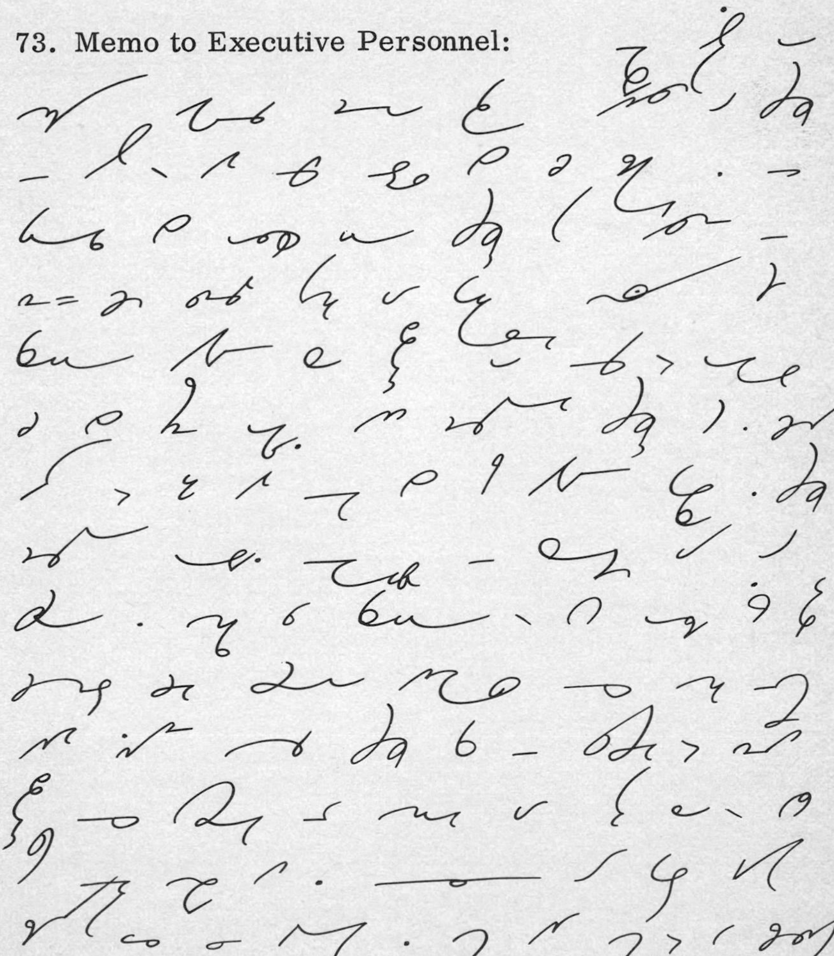

74. To the Faculty:

(shorthand) 14

---

75. Inventory and Sales Personnel:

(shorthand) 30

DON'T LET THIS HAPPEN TO YOU!

DICTATED

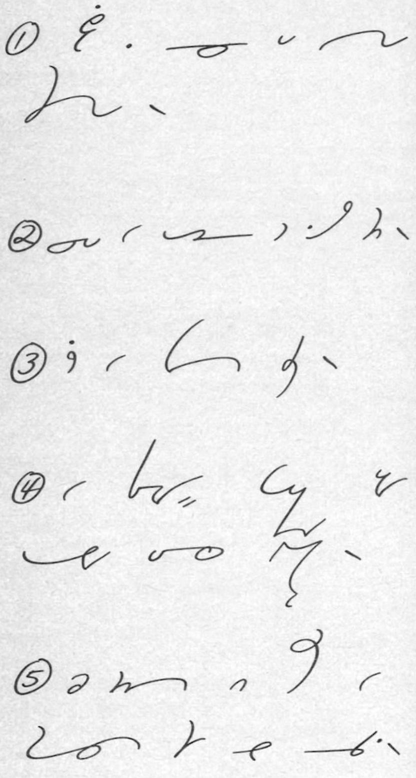

1. He was a man of great vigor.

2. I know the room is handy for you.

3. He is the big chief.

4. The Johnston project was the least of my troubles.

5. We suggest you save the flag for the next meeting.

TRANSCRIBED

1. He was a man of great figure.

2. I know the room is empty for you.

3. He is the big cheese.

4. The Johnston project was the last of my troubles.

5. We suggest you wave the flag for the next meeting.

LESSON 16

PRINCIPLES

Lessons 16 through 20 will include another type of review. The first letter or article of Lessons 16-20 will emphasize brief forms and words of high frequency; the remainder of the Reading and Self-Dictation Practice exercises will review the principles. The following chart includes all the vowels and vowel joinings.

1					
2					
3					
4					
5					
6					
7					
8					
9					
10					
11					
12					
13					

1. mail, revival, group, piano, choice, approximately.
2. period, dates, accompanied, know, number, area.

3. annoyance, quota, Owens, practice, ringing, doorbell.
4. production, create, twice, drawee, kindly, little.
5. law, wages, buyers, proud, quickly, radio.
6. replenished, solved, worry, prior, Edwin, bureau.
7. appliance, operettas, pair, holding, first, appreciate.
8. review, yes, announcement, seats, healthy, swift.
9. violin, unite, association, agenda, charter, grouped.
10. switching, ahead, power, yarn, Shakespearian, hurry.
11. formula, while, aware, dispute, Yale, initiate.
12. pave, firm, previous, winter, away, how.
13. prices, rayon, family, fabric, watch, teacher.

FREQUENTLY USED WORDS

Here are 40 additional words of high frequency.

1. wish, card, paid, sure, interested, without.
2. interest, further, member, general, material, money.
3. customers, upon, come, him, job, own.
4. future, feel, given, report, able, write.
5. forward, week, received, additional, board, division.
6. subject, receive, sent, above, soon, dealers.
7. request, income, until, advise.

READING AND SELF-DICTATION PRACTICE

76. Dear Mrs. Ramos:

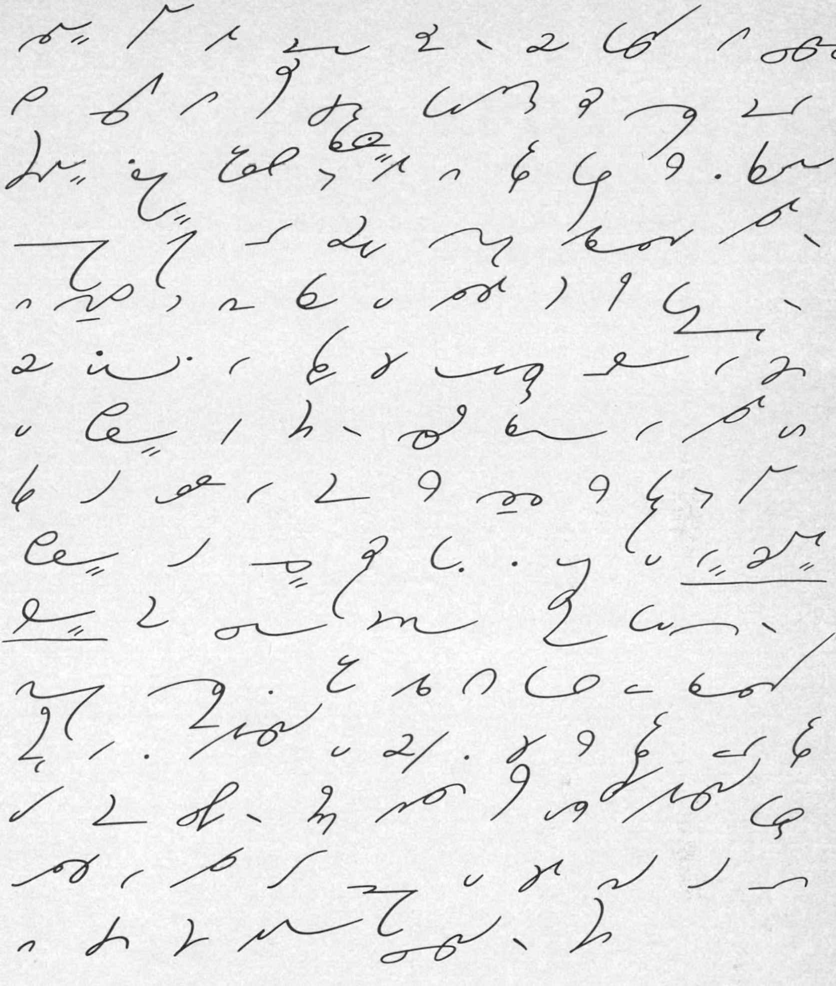

(shorthand text)

---

77. To the Members of the Violin Club:

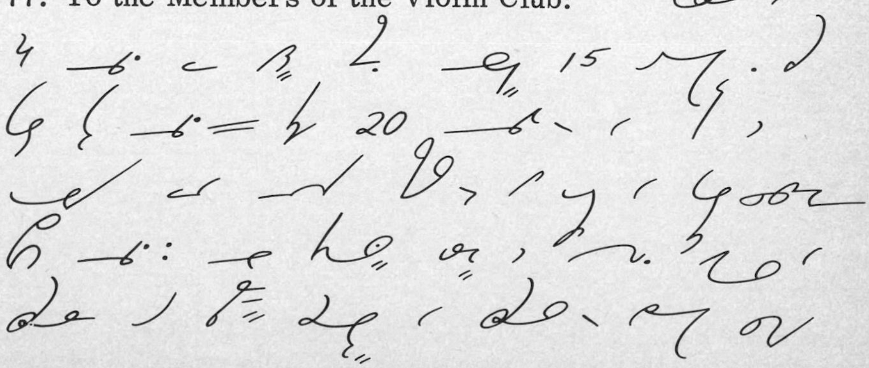

(shorthand text)

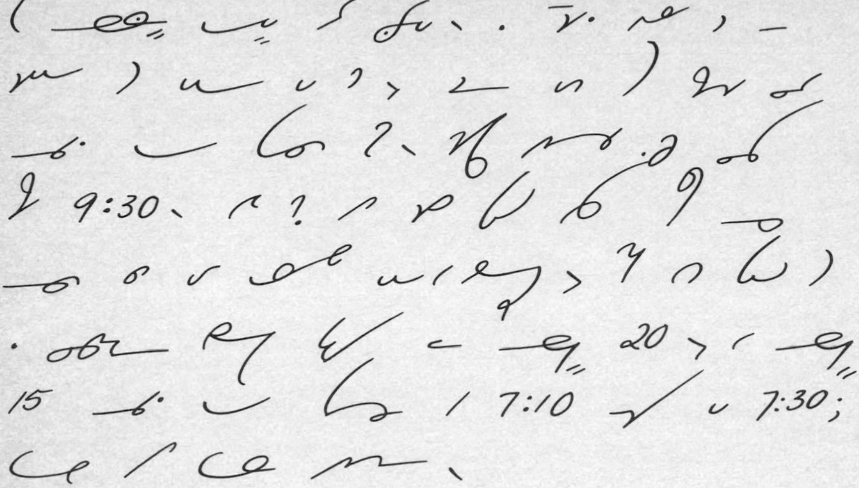

78. Miss Freeman:

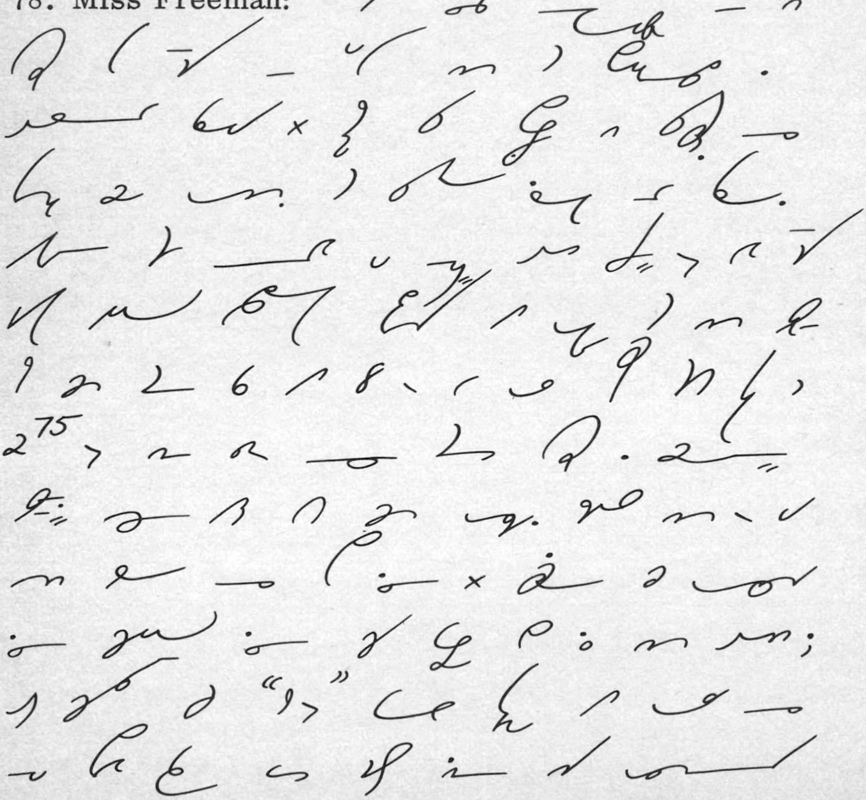

(shorthand)

---

79. Dear Mr. Powers:

(shorthand)

LESSON 17

PRINCIPLES

The following chart contains all the <u>joined</u> word beginnings.

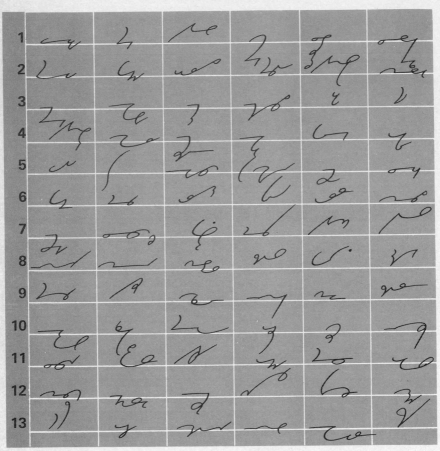

1. almost, furnish, dismiss, convention, inefficiency, emergency.
2. furlough, pursuit, already, furniture, describe, commerce.
3. information, impressed, enforce, unfortunately, also, further.
4. description, complete, investment, impossible, permission, report.
5. although, before, mistake, competent, unfair, emotion.
6. person, submit, reduce, beyond, return, committee.
7. unfinished, immaculately, perhaps, submitted, discuss, delay.
8. include, comment, unnecessary, extra, pertaining, substantial.

9. forget, decision, concern, encourage, unknown, extreme.
10. misplace, suburb, formal, receive, confess, engage.
11. enact, explain, decide, result, foreman, reply.
12. connection, insurance, emphasis, ultimate, begin, consult.
13. forever, receipt, construct, increase, employment, afforded.

FREQUENTLY USED WORDS

Here are 40 additional words of high frequency.

1. cordially, offer, supply, public, invoice, too.
2. held, opportunity, shipment, believe, attached, book.
3. while, right, enclosing, rates, name, total.
4. payment, federal, area, increase, past, why.
5. defense, back, equipment, items, loan, better.
6. secretary, again, making, free, going, months.
7. membership, group, copies, men.

READING AND SELF-DICTATION PRACTICE

80. Dear Mr. Johnson:

[Shorthand text]

---

81. Dear Miss Carter: *[Shorthand text]*

82. Dear Mr. Conroy: *[shorthand]*

[shorthand lines]

---

83. THE COMPETENT SECRETARY SAVES THE EMPLOYER'S TIME *[shorthand]*

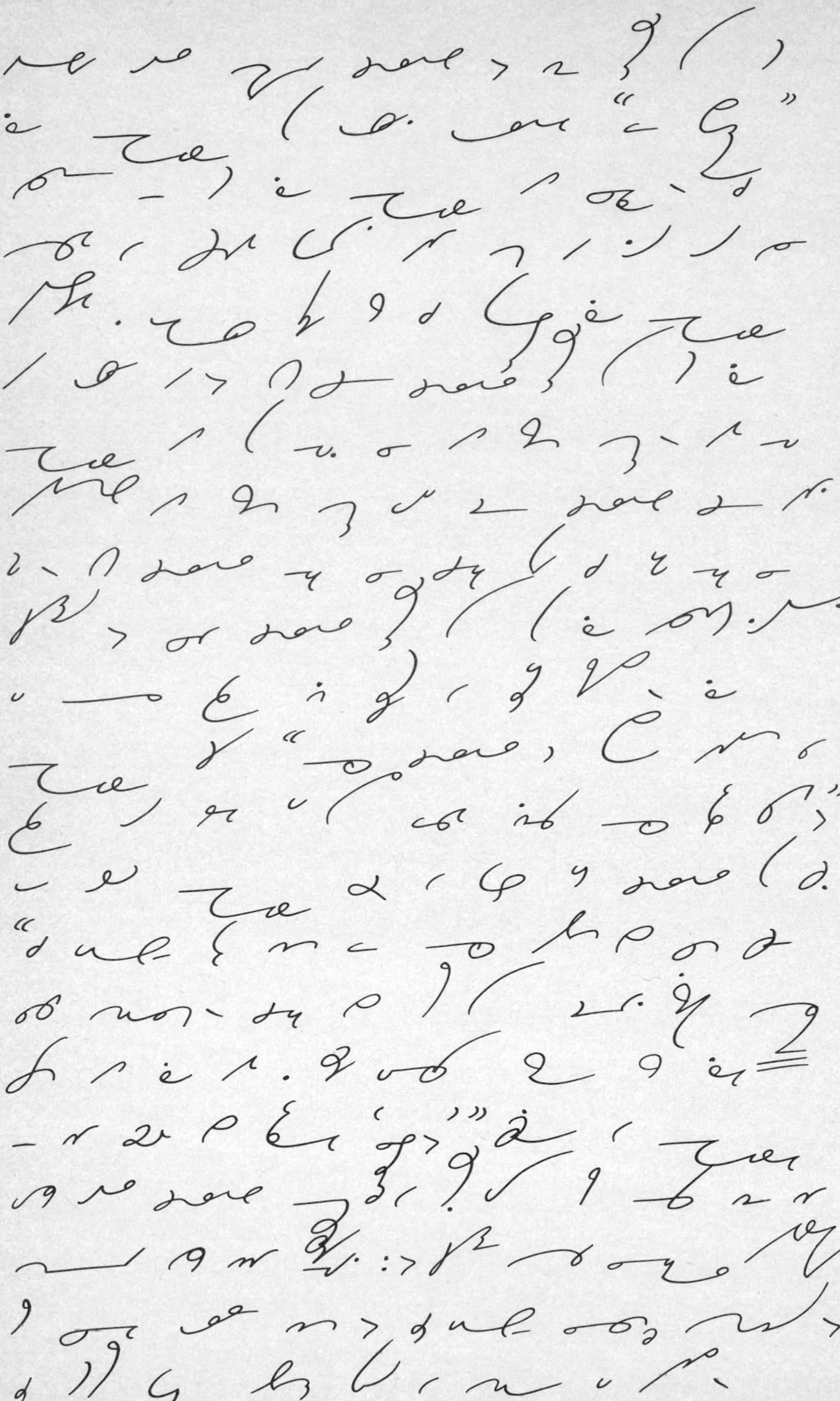

LESSON 18

PRINCIPLES

The following chart contains all the <u>joined</u> word endings.

1						
2						
3						
4						
5						
6						
7						
8						
9						
10						
11						
12						
13						

1. action, daily, beneficial, modern, verified, annual.
2. pressure, Pittsfield, application, extremely, possible, western.
3. family, actual, results, deficient, collection, managed.
4. payment, northern, together, bother, schedule, Bridgeport.
5. occasion, easily, adjustment, recently, entitled, obtain.
6. actually, admission, operation, readily, accomplishment, attain.
7. shortly, yourself, Stamford, Zanesville, efficient, especially.
8. statement, retain, assume, themselves, Hartford, Newburgh.
9. patient, locally, reasonable, helpful, consume, picture.

10. Harrisburg, Princeton, efficiency, essential, acceptable, hopeful.
11. presume, lecture, Allentown, package, official, clearly.
12. advisable, useful, presumption, nature, Jacksonville, myself.
13. currently, initial, desirable, department, resumed, secured.

FREQUENTLY USED WORDS

Here are 40 additional words of high frequency.

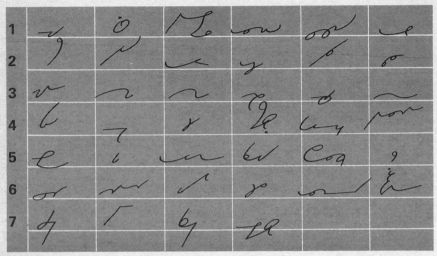

1. note, high, delivery, record, account, less.
2. ever, don't, long, receipt, did, within.
3. water, go, great, keep, night, glad.
4. both, important, set, advertising, promotion, director.
5. national, show, local, period, application, ease.
6. another, contract, orders, city, recommend, hospital.
7. change, done, charge, merchandise.

READING AND SELF-DICTATION PRACTICE

84. Dear Member:

[Shorthand text]

---

85. Dear Miss Strong:

[Shorthand text]

86. Dear Mr. Orlando: 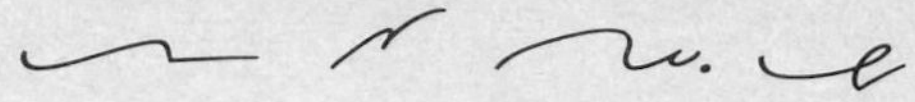

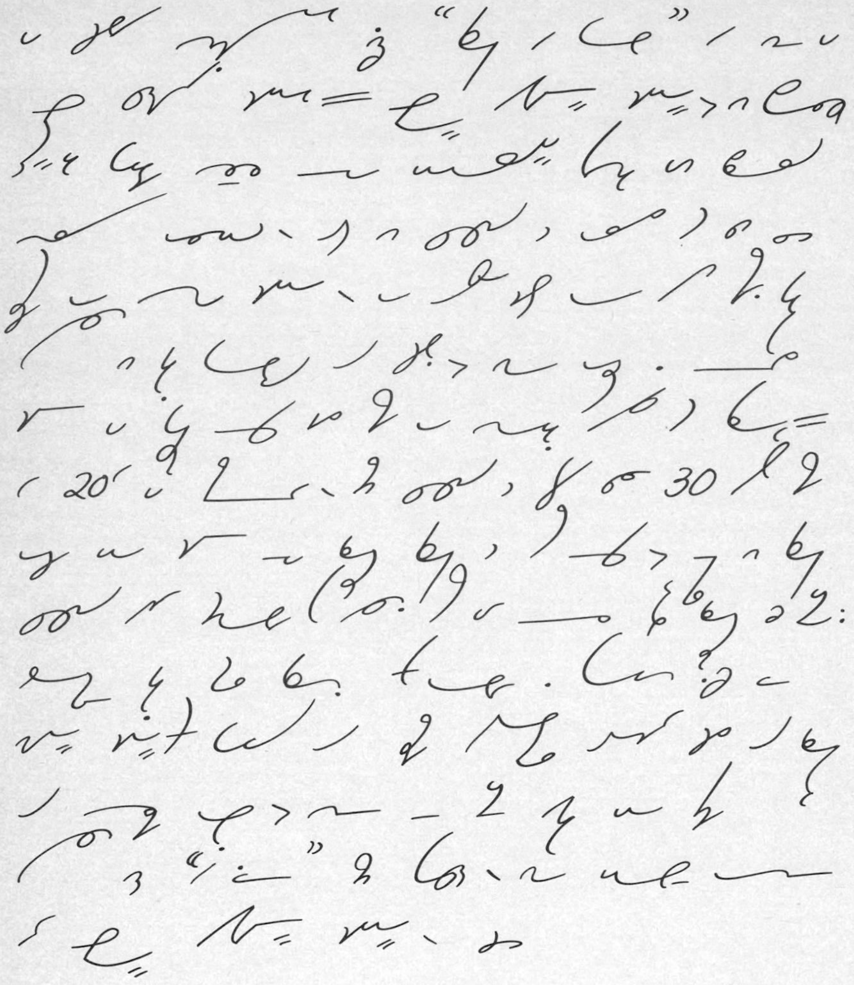

87. Dear Mr. Adams: 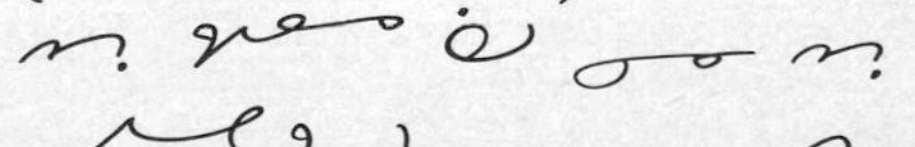

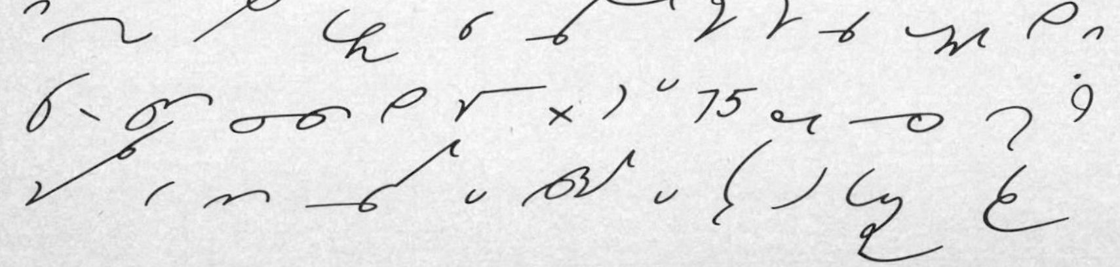

[Shorthand text]

14

15

12

88. Gentlemen:

LESSON 19

PRINCIPLES

The following chart contains all the <u>disjoined</u> word beginnings and endings.

1. self-evident, international, interests, transferred, undergone, justification.
2. anything, neighborhood, self-satisfied, introduce, postcard, translation.
3. article, something, knowingly, childhood, self-educated, introductory.
4. postpone, transcribe, critical, program, meetings, security.
5. circumstances, entered, postal, transact, clerical, monogram.
6. proceedings, familiarity, unselfishness, enterprise, superb, overlook.
7. technical, authority, accumulation, entertain, circulate, circulation.

8. superior, oversight, ownership, maturity, congratulations, electric.
9. electrical, electrically, supervision, overcoming, membership, abilities.
10. stimulated, introduction, electric wire, offerings, supervisor, overdue.
11. relationship, facility, tabulation, Framingham, interfere, selfish.
12. entrance, understood, notification, faculty, afterward, Wellington.
13. interference, interrupt, interruption, understand, specifications, loyalty.

FREQUENTLY USED WORDS

Here is another group of 40 words of high frequency.

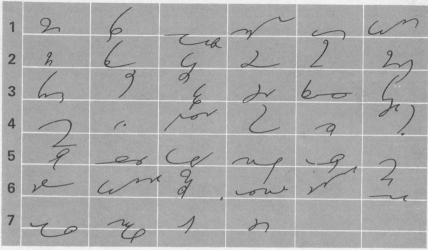

1. ask, basis, employees, customer, organization, production.
2. issue, bill, purchase, fill, even, effective.
3. books, several, position, fact, chairman, benefits.
4. government, think, direct, value, cash, having.
5. type, market, pleased, college, life, convention.
6. still, products, association, records, students, Mrs.
7. reply, cooperation, therefore, section.

READING AND SELF-DICTATION PRACTICE

89. Dear Mr. Cunningham:

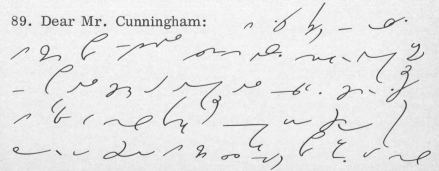

90. Dear Mrs. Wellington:

91. Dear Bob:

92. Mr. Perez:

372

---

93. Dear Mr. Murdock:

LESSON 20

PRINCIPLES

The following chart contains all the blends and illustrates the omission of vowels and consonants.

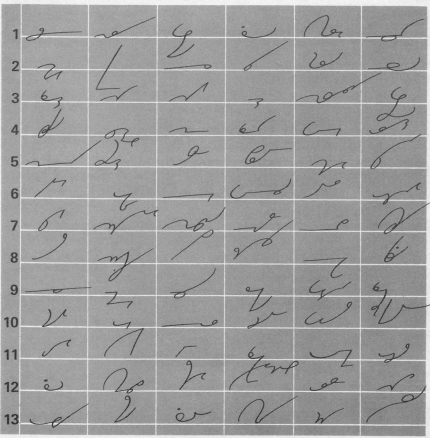

1. examine, credit, prevent, held, difference, maintain.
2. competition, judgment, money, edit, friend, mailed.
3. serious, contain, condition, news, graduated, prevailed.
4. giant, accessories, come, certain, permission, reduce.
5. commented, various, entire, appointment, confidence, attempt.
6. donation, report, mention, permanent, entry, residents.
7. attention, customers, ground, modern, monthly, divided.

8. empty, cultivated, today, estimated, member, behind.
9. minimum, information, named, urgent, persistent, services.
10. funds, rush, memory, center, promptly, gentle.
11. audience, damage, ton, suburban, luncheon, recently.
12. heard, definitely, evidence, demonstration, return, continue.
13. listed, event, harder, devoted, sudden, demand.

FREQUENTLY USED WORDS

Here is the last group of 40 words of high frequency.

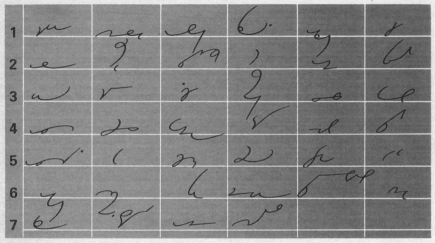

1. store, commerce, large, building, reserve, sheet.
2. real, savings, education, four, reason, bonds.
3. old, statement, whether, average, immediately, place.
4. regular, family, personal, system, notice, addition.
5. regarding, put, weeks, field, power, thanks.
6. representative, covering, box, small, administration, once.
7. sale, assistant, room, country.

READING AND SELF-DICTATION PRACTICE

94. SECRETARIAL ATTRIBUTES

95. Dear Mrs. Gentry:

96. Dear Neighbor:

97. Dear Alumnus:

98. Dear Mrs. Bennett:

[shorthand outlines]

---

99. Dear Mr. Powers: *[shorthand outlines]*

[several lines of shorthand outlines]

WHERE TO FROM HERE?

Now that you have completed a comprehensive review of the principles of Gregg Shorthand, you are ready to further enhance that skill through a dictation practice program.

The ability to take verbatim office dictation, according to a research conducted by Dr. H. H. Green, requires a "cruising" speed of 80 to 100 words a minute, with speed spurts between 120 and 140 words a minute. To be certain of a "new matter" speed of 100 words a minute, you will want to bring your speed on practiced material — letters or articles that you have previously read in shorthand or recorded dictation that you have taken several times — to at least 120 words a minute.

Remember that the greater dictation speed you attain the greater the confidence you will have In your ability, and the better you will perform.

DON'T LET THIS HAPPEN TO YOU!

DICTATED	TRANSCRIBED

1. Please collect the papers and leave them in the basket.

2. It was evident that he was jeering the crowd.

3. The label was not secure on the box.

4. He lived in Newburgh most of that period.

5. The package arrived too late.

1. Please correct the papers and leave them in the basket.

2. It was evident that he was cheering the crowd.

3. The wrapper was not secure on the box.

4. He lived in Newport most of that period.

5. The baggage arrived too late.

KEY TO READING AND
SELF-DICTATION PRACTICE

(The material is counted in groups of 20 standard words or 28 syllables for convenience in timing the reading or dictation.)

Lesson 1, Page 2

1. Mr. Hale: May I bring in my car for repairs one day during the coming week? There are several things that need[1] to be done, and I have been lax in taking care of them. I know that I need a new spare tire, for the old one is[2] so worn that it must be replaced. Too, there are a number of chips in the paint that need to be looked after. The[3] important thing, however, is that you fix the brakes. I cannot drive the car in its present condition. As you know,[4] my territory includes all of James County. Many of the roads in this county are not paved, and on steep grades[5] driving can be dangerous.

Would you check with the mechanic to find out whether there is any chance that I might[6] have this work done on Wednesday, May 27? I should like to know so that I can make my plans. If the work will[7] take longer than a day to finish, then I shall have to hire a car in order to cover my territory.[8]

Please let me hear from you soon. Perhaps you would like to telephone me, or you may write me if you wish. I will be[9] at home the rest of this week. Cordially yours, (188)

2. Dear Harry: Could you give me the names and addresses of the people who will be staying at the Clear Lake Motel[1] during our club meeting beginning March 15? I must mail their reservations for rooms immediately. I[2] believe the motel will give us a special rate of $7 plus tax. This rate seems reasonable, don't you[3] agree? All rooms are with bath and telephone.

Are the papers which you were to prepare being typed? I am relying[4] on you to have them ready for the meeting. I know it is not an easy job, and I am glad that no one[5] gave it to me! Will you be able to attend the meetings? It will help a great deal if you are there, as you are[6] perhaps the only one who will be able to answer all the questions that may be asked.

I am attaching the[7] list of new members that Mary Grady gave me. Have you seen it? Did you know that she is writing a history[8] of the club? George (163)

3. Dear Sir: Your most important asset is your health. Are you taking good care of it? Or, like many others, are you[1] putting off having a health examination because you feel the bill will be too high? If so, we have good news[2] for you.

Our new Three-Way Health Plan does three important things for you: It gives you a thorough examination three[3] times each year by skilled doctors; it gives you home treatment when you need it; and it provides complete hospital benefits.[4] This new plan has become so well known that more than ten thousand people have joined it during the last three months. Yet[5] the fees are very small.

The enclosed booklet explains the plan fully. You owe it to yourself to take an hour[6] to read it carefully. Why not telephone us this week and arrange to visit our office so that we can explain[7] more completely the benefits of joining the Three-Way Plan. You will be glad you did. Cordially yours, (158)

4. Dear Sir: Do you take chances when you drive? "Of course not!" you say, but each one of us takes chances when we are not[1] prepared for winter driving.

The smart driver does not take chances when driving in sleet, ice, or snow. He would make sure he[2] has a set of Atlas chains in his car during the winter season.

The car owner who has Atlas chains knows that[3] he will not need to worry even in the worst weather. These chains snap on easily, and they grip icy roads like[4] a vise—no fear of accidents or delays.

Please look at the attached report on drivers who have used Atlas chains.[5] Do not take unnecessary risks. Get your set of Atlas chains today. Cordially yours, (115)

5. To Branch Managers: You all did such a good job at the party last Friday that I wish to take this way of thanking[1] each of you. I never saw a more willing and eager team.

I would like particularly to comment on[2]

the decorations; the effect was so startling that I thought they were arranged by a professional. Mrs. Perez[3] said she would like to take lessons in flower arrangements from the decoration committee.

The food was so[4] beautifully displayed that it would have given anyone an appetite. A number of our guests thought that we had[5] a caterer supply the food. When I told them that you people had done everything, they could scarcely believe it.[6] So thanks once more. F. C. Perez (125)

Lesson 2, Page 7

6. Dear Madam: When may we have the opportunity of showing you our new Store-Away filing cabinets for[1] the home? Perhaps you saw them advertised in the *Daily News* on Wednesday and Thursday of last week. They will be on[2] display at the Wilson branch of our store, 226 Broadway, on Friday, November 7.

Those who have seen these[3] smart filing cabinets have expressed delight with their beauty and efficiency. You will be pleased, too, with their modern[4] styling. And what is more, they do not waste space; they save space for you. The manufacturers have made files for[5] many years. Businessmen all over the country have purchased them. We feel fortunate that we should be the first in the[6] city to feature these files, which are designed expressly for the home.

A special demonstration of these files will[7] be given on Friday at 2:30 p.m. I hope you will be able to come for at least a quick visit.[8] Cordially yours, (163)

7. Dear Mr. Wade: We are pleased to send you the sales analysis that we have just completed, using the figures[1] that you supplied us recently. We sincerely hope that we have set up this information the way you want it.[2] If we have not, it is essential that we hear from you not later than Tuesday of next week in order to make[3] any changes in time for your board meeting.

As for the additional material that was promised you, we[4] will get it to you before the end of December. Please be patient with us. Very truly yours, (97)

8. Dear Mr. Wooley: Your copy of our fall advertising bulletin is in the mail. We feel that this year's[1] bulletin is much better than any we have ever had before. We feel sure that you will like the special features[2] that appear at the end of each section.

We take pride in the fact that during the past fifty years we have been able[3] to supply our bulletin at a very low price. However, this particular issue is the first that[4] we have been able to offer for less than 75 cents. You will be glad to learn that we can supply you[5] with any number you wish.

To be assured of getting your copies while they are still available, Mr. Wooley,[6] fill in the enclosed form and return it to us quickly. Your order will receive prompt action. Yours truly,[7] (140)

9. Dear Mrs. Quimby: You are invited to the grand opening of our new store at noon on Monday. Our business[1] has grown so much in the past two years that we have had to move to larger, more efficient quarters. Our new location[2] is at 125 Queens Boulevard.

All types of woolens are to be featured on the opening day; the[3] second day we will feature nylons and dacrons; the third day we will emphasize accessories of all kinds.

The[4] enclosed picture story will give you a partial idea of just what we have planned. We also have some delightful[5] surprises that we would rather not mention at this time. Come and find out for yourself!

We hope that you will be able[6] to join us on Monday, June 16. Sincerely yours, (129)

10. Dear Cousin Carol: In my previous letter to you I said that, on the whole, I like this vacation spot[1] better than any other I have ever visited. The mornings and nights are very cool; the days are warm but not[2] hot. I have only five precious days left, and I shall be sorry when my vacation ends.

When I get home, I'll explain[3] to you and Bruce Moore why I did not come back last Saturday for the Social Club dance. It's a long story. Did[4] I tell you that Homer and Bill drove up here last Sunday? Homer borrowed his sister's car for the trip.

Don't wait long[5] to drop me a line. I do want to hear from you again. Sincerely, (113)

11. Dear Sir: I should like to show you how to improve the businesslike appearance of your flower shop with a well-planned[1] driveway.

Please look over the photos of some driveways we have installed in the past two years. Then check with the owners[2] of these shops as to their satisfaction with our work.

Mr. Quail, of The Flower Garden, for example, will be[3] glad to give you an endorsement. He is very well pleased with the improvement and resulting increase in business.[4] Yours very truly, (84)

Lesson 3, Page 12

12. Dear Mr. Field: Perhaps some of your friends are planning to retire at 60 with a monthly income of[1] $500. Do you think you

will be able to do so, too—or will you barely manage to get by? Research shows[2] that surprisingly few people—less than 20 percent—plan ahead for retirement. It will be to your advantage[3] to start saving toward retirement now, and we can help you.

After you have had a chance to study the features[4] of our retirement plan described in the enclosure, we shall be glad to receive a telephone call to arrange[5] for a personal meeting. You will be under no obligation whatsoever. Cordially yours, (104)

13. Dear Mr. Arnold: There is a new family insurance plan—offered for the first time in January—that[1] is causing much excitement among those who hear about it.

Do you know it is possible for your entire[2] family to be covered under a single protection plan? Any new child in your family will be[3] insured as soon as he is ten days old, and there will be no increase in the rates thereafter, no matter how many[4] children you have. I think you will readily see that this is a totally new concept in family[5] insurance.

Please do not make the mistake of waiting until trouble arrives. It will be well worth your while to invite[6] our representative, Mr. Childs, to call on you to describe the unique features of this insurance[7] plan. He will gladly do so if you will telephone him—the number is 642-4121. Cordially[8] yours, (161)

14. Dear Mr. Ramos: I am very glad to send you our new catalogue describing the latest models of the[1] Cold King coolers. We have the finest low-priced coolers on the market. The Neptune retails for only[2] $16.95; the North Wind, for $22.95. Over 3,000 of these coolers[3] have already been sold.

We are glad to be able to offer you a special discount of 25 percent[4] instead of your usual 20 percent on all Cold King coolers. This discount is available only[5] during the months of February, March, and April; therefore, you must act quickly.

Over 3,000 customers[6] can't be wrong. Order your supply of Cold King coolers today, and get ready for the big May through August business.[7] Sincerely yours, (143)

15. Dear Subscriber: We wrote you early in June that we would be glad to renew your subscription to *United[1] Business* and delay billing until July.

We sent the bill in July, but we have not yet heard from you. We know you[2] have not ignored our correspondence. More likely, this small bill has slipped your mind.

If the check has been mailed, please ignore[3] this reminder. If it has not, may we

have your check in the enclosed envelope? Cordially yours, (77)

16. Dear Mr. Kenmore: During September and October we are making a drive to help the "economically[1] disadvantaged" in this area. A corresponding campaign will be conducted in another part of[2] the country in November and December.

If three million people would donate $3 each, a nine million[3] dollar fund could be established. Think of the many socially important activities that could be conducted[4] with money of this kind. If three million school children would add ten cents each, another $300,000[5] would be added.

We could look for a decrease in social decay that results from slum areas. As you know,[6] early training in socially correct habits is an important step in this direction.

Most of our slum[7] areas have developed because buildings were not properly repaired and maintained. Mostly, some people will claim, this[8] resulted from inertia on the part of the tenants. In a few hundred cases that were retraced after[9] families were moved into better neighborhoods, it was found that the degrading atmosphere in which they formerly[10] lived was responsible for their earlier carelessness. When they moved into a well-kept neighborhood, they became[11] aware of their social responsibilities.

What do we want you to do? We want you to place a check[12] or money order in the envelope enclosed. Then drop it into the mailbox promptly. You will, won't you? Cordially[13] yours, (261)

Lesson 4, Page 17

17. Dear Mr. Franklin: On Tuesday, August 10, I shall be meeting with Keith Yale from Cleveland. Mr. Yale, who was one[1] of your students at Chicago Junior College, is applying for a position in our bank's bookkeeping[2] department. His school record is highly satisfactory, and we thank you for sending it. Would you also answer[3] a few questions concerning him? Please be very frank.

Did he get along well with the teachers and others in your[4] school? Was he able to take criticism? Did he turn in his work on time? Was his attendance satisfactory?[5] Was he a hard worker?

We shall keep any information you give us in strict confidence, of course. Cordially[6] yours, (121)

18. Dear Mrs. Jackson: The national convention of the Yachting Association meets at the Overman[1] Hotel in New Orleans on May

16 and 17. Delegates from every chapter in the country will attend.[2] The delegates from Michigan and Pennsylvania planned the program; Oregon and New York delegates are in[3] charge of social activities, which will feature sports events. The Los Angeles committee has planned the banquet.[4]

Your chapter has not yet expressed a desire to participate in any activity on the schedule.[5] Won't you look over the accompanying list and let us know your preferences? We particularly need help with the[6] yacht races and other sports events. Perhaps one of your members would sing the national anthem at the banquet.[7]

I shall be looking forward to hearing from you soon. Thank you very much. Cordially yours, (156)

19. Dear Mr. Singer: I accompanied my mother when she rented the apartment at Yellow Ridge. We both[1] believed that a new sink would be installed, and that she would have a section of the yard for a small garden. Actually,[2] these are two matters of great importance to her.

If your company does not yield with respect to the yard and[3] sink, I am sure my mother will break her lease. I am, therefore, bringing your failure to keep to the actual terms[4] of the lease to your attention.

Please let me know right away what we can expect. Yours truly, (96)

20. Dear Mr. Lopez: As editor of *Youth Forum* I endeavor to schedule some nature articles in[1] each volume. Among the most popular have been those featuring our national parks. Yellowstone was the best ever.[2] I have not been successful in securing a series to equal it.

Do you think you could deliver a[3] series equally as good? I would suggest either our native animals or reptiles. Neither has had[4] previous coverage.

As you are aware, we schedule our articles many months ahead. Please let me know whether[5] you can gather the material and pictures for our next volume. I would like to have your "yes" when I return[6] from Boston next week. Cordially yours, (127)

21. Dear Mr. Didham: Have you been satisfied with the leather yokes you have been purchasing in recent years for your[1] cattle? We can help you overcome the bother of shopping around, particularly since there are so few[2] sources from which quality harness is available.

Full descriptions in the accompanying catalog will help[3] you select the proper yokes for your animals. The various types of yokes are listed under breed headings to[4] greatly simplify selection of the proper type.

Return the order blank with the proper serial numbers[5] listed. If your check is sent with the order, take a 5 percent cash discount. Cordially yours, (118)

Lesson 5, Page 21

22. Dear Mr. Weeks: As one of our valued stockholders, you are entitled to know the latest development in[1] the Universal Brush Company.

Recently we merged with the World Products Corporation. I realize that there[2] are those groups who warn small companies of the dangers of bigness—that it is likely to weaken our position.[3] I do not understand this theory, for we have already made progress. We feel that with this merger we will[4] automatically have many advantages:

1. It will enable our customers to choose from a wider[5] variety of products.

2. Fast, courteous treatment of all customers will be possible.

3. We have more[6] capital with which to expand our systems, services, and operations.

4. In this merger we have acquired[7] many outstanding people. As you know, we have always wanted wider market coverage, and this expansion[8] of personnel will certainly give it to us.

5. Faster methods of shipment will be available to us.[9] Distance is no longer a problem, and damaged merchandise should be cut to a minimum.

On the basis of[10] this evidence, I am sure you will agree that we did a wise thing. We estimate that our volume will more than[11] double in the coming year. Yes, we are getting big, and we hope to get even bigger.

I hope you will be[12] pleased with this new development at Universal. We have gone to a great deal of trouble to make sure it was[13] the right thing for us to do. After the coming year you can judge for yourself. As always, we welcome your reactions.[14] Individual stockholders are, after all, the people who are most concerned. We shall be glad to hear from you if you[15] wish to offer any suggestions. Sincerely yours, (310)

23. Dear Mrs. Swift: They say that if you want to get something done, give it to a busy person. As usual, we[1] are looking to you for leadership.

The first PTA meeting of the year will be held at Freedom High School[2] October 10—next Thursday evening. It will be divided into two parts—a one-hour general business session[3] beginning at 7:30, and a "fun hour" will follow.

We particularly need your guidance and[4] opinions at the business session. We are attempting to organize several committees for the summer. Because[5] of your experience in committee work, we hope you will be able to assist us at this organization[6] meeting.

During the last hour you can sit back with the audience and enjoy the fun, as the teachers are putting[7] on a skit called "Just Between Us."

May I please have your acceptance? Please call me at 413-1612,[8] Extension 21, or use the enclosed envelope for your reply. Sincerely yours, (176)

24. Dear Mrs. Lane: Thank you for your recent letter inviting me to participate in the PTA meeting[1] on October 10 at Freedom High School. My answer is "yes."

I have several important suggestions, which I[2] would like to talk over with you in your office some morning before October 10, as it is difficult to[3] outline them in a letter.

I have been seriously interested for many years in the field of mental[4] health. Mental disease in young people is a terrible problem, and treatment is slow and expensive. I would,[5] therefore, be genuinely pleased to have the opportunity to work on this committee. If you can use[6] additional workers who appreciate the importance of serving on this committee, I have several names[7] to propose. Sincerely yours, P.S. By the way, Mr. Swift will be at the meeting with me. (157)

25. To the Staff: Good news! In the future Washington's Birthday, February 22, will be a holiday.[1] Since it falls on a Sunday this year, we shall be observing the holiday on Monday. We wanted to get this[2] bulletin to you in advance so that you might plan for the long weekend.

We have been asked by the Travel Club[3] to announce that arrangements are being made for a trip to Mountain Springs. You must have your reservation in by[4] February 10. To obtain further information, call Miss Summers on Extension 2651. J. H. Harris[5] (100)

26. Dear Mr. Jones: Will you please check my account? I cannot seem to straighten out my records.

I seldom forget to[1] make a record of a payment on the account, but so far as I can ascertain, there is one payment not[2] recorded. If that is a fact, the account would have been in balance.

On June 10 I sent a check for $50[3] issued to me by Random Enterprises, which I had endorsed over to your store. Perhaps this ac-

counts for the[4] error. Very truly yours, (85)

Lesson 6, Page 27

27. Dear Mr. Royal: As a merchant, you are, of course, proud of the progress that is now being made in road improvement[1] in the entire state, as well as in Minneapolis. These better roads will bring more business to Minneapolis[2] and you want to have a part in it.

We would like you to study the United Merchandising Plan. Its[3] purpose is to help you sell more at less expense. Here are just a few of our services:

1. We maintain a staff[4] who will see that your windows are trimmed each month.

2. You can use our credit to purchase additional merchandise.[5]

3. You'll save on printing costs the United way.

4. We have an outlet store that will relieve you of soiled merchandise[6] at a reasonable discount.

Why not take a few minutes to read our offer. If, after a careful study[7] of the details, you wish to have any of these services explained more fully, we shall send one of our[8] representatives to tell you about the progress you can make the United way.

If you feel no further explanation[9] is needed, the enclosed contract signed by you is all that is necessary—we'll do the rest. Yours truly,[10] (200)

28. Dear Roy: If my memory is correct, I failed to mention that I am staying in Philadelphia longer[1] than I planned. There has been some kind of difficulty with our land here.

A few of the tenants claimed they had not signed[2] their leases because a study made by the city council might result in a widening of the street. In that[3] event, they explained, they thought some units of the property might be sold.

I doubt that was the reason, but I find[4] it difficult and annoying to handle such details. Ordinarily, I take care of such matters myself;[5] but today I have retained a real estate firm and ordered them to look into the difficulty.

As I mentioned[6] to you, I plan to go on to Detroit and then to Toledo to review the progress that has been made in[7] maintaining family properties in those cities. Then I will go on to California.

As soon as I[8] return to my office, I'll send you a short memo for publication on the restrictions the public must observe[9] during the current water shortage. Cordially yours, (190)

29. Dear Mr. Vargas: You inquired about our Alabama link-chain fence. As described in the booklet I sent[1] you, this fence is more secure than the ordinary fence. Why? It is much heavier and is treated to withstand[2] the elements. This means that you can trust it to keep your children inside and stray animals outside.

As to its[3] purchase—that's easy. The enclosed brochure explains the monthly time-payment plan. If you place your order promptly, you[4] will be exempt from monthly payments until fall.

This fence is one you will be proud to own; and in addition to[5] its attractive appearance, it requires very little maintenance.

Don't let another minute go by without[6] considering the difficulties that could be prevented by putting up an Alabama link-chain fence.[7] Cordially yours, (144)

30. Ralph Shorter: There has been some difficulty in finding a salesman for Missouri and Nebraska. Why not speak[1] to John Tenant. He would like a change in territory.

How much of a salary would be in order? If an[2] offer has been made to someone else and refused, the salary established might make it possible for you to[3] speak to Mr. Tenant with a good chance of his accepting.

Please act upon this recommendation immediately[4] and let me know the result. Howard Standish (89)

Lesson 7, Page 31

31. Dear Mr. Bryan: Several leading citizens feel that we should pursue a trial promotion campaign to[1] attract more industry to this southern area. We are, therefore, organizing a committee to work on the[2] project. May we count on you? If so, will it be permissible to use your name?

If we are going to do[3] something to protect our town's future by bringing modern industry here, we need to organize a plan and place[4] advertisements in the newspapers and other media. We can use your ideas as an advertising director[5] to put this campaign across everywhere throughout the state.

For the present, we want you to help us create a[6] workable plan. Before the funds requested will be approved, everyone will want to know what our plans are.

If for[7] any reason your regular work might bias your action or create a problem, can you suggest someone else[8] to whom we could turn? Cordially yours, (167)

32. To the Staff: An envelope containing a quantity of color swatches and patterns for ladies' purses,[1] identified by folio numbers, was lost sometime this morning. We believe the loss occurred somewhere in the[2] rayon building; possibly on the first floor.

If it is not located within a day or two, we probably will[3] not be able to meet one of the terms of a quotation: to match the colors perfectly.

I am requesting[4] everyone to check his work station at once. The package represents a big loss if it is not located. If[5] you find it, report immediately to Julia Kane. Her extension is 613. John Barton (117)

33. Dear Miss Porter: In an effort to bring greater appreciation of modern poetry and music to the[1] public, your local radio station will soon offer a new program. We hope it will become a permanent[2] feature.

In order to determine its appeal, we should appreciate your bringing it to the attention of[3] your students, and reporting their interest to us. May we ask in addition that you permit us to send a[4] speaker to your school each week to give your students advance information and greater appreciation of each[5] program? We think the students will find this most worthwhile.

We will, of course, continue our science series and will grant[6] permission for students to take part in the program. There is one condition, however. We never permit[7] students in the studio without passes, but you may request passes in whatever quantities you need to make[8] it possible for everybody to attend. Probably you should ask for an additional supply so[9] nobody will be turned away.

If you have any questions, or if you wish to suggest some program ideas that will[10] help us to make the radio station a greater asset to the schools in this area, be sure to let us know.[11] Cordially yours, (223)

34. Dear Mr. Brierly: The price quoted by our representative for the toaster was not correct. The enclosed[1] copy of a newspaper advertisement published throughout the state verifies that this appliance has been[2] advertised everywhere at $21. Your wholesale price would, therefore, be $12.60 in dozen[3] lots.

We stated in our contract that ordering in dozen quantities is a condition of sale.

Notwithstanding[4] the fact that a responsible company representative gave you different price information, we[5] must keep to the regular terms outlined in our dealer reports, which you receive regularly.

This is a somewhat[6] embarrassing situation, but we are confident with this explanation you will withdraw your request[7] for rebilling. Cordially yours, P.S. We are researching the possibility of having a larger[8] thermostatic control for future models and will send you the information as soon as we have a complete report.[9] (180)

35. Dear Mr. Turner: When I was on vacation in your state, I purchased chances on a car. I have the stubs of[1] the ones I bought.

Recently I learned that I had won the car. However, I have never been notified to that[2] effect nor have I been advised where to claim it.

I have written to the organization that sold the chances[3] but have not had a reply.

I expect I need an attorney in such a situation and I am writing[4] to see if you will represent me. Cordially yours, (90)

36. Dear Mr. Sanchez: With your permission, I have turned over to your attorney a medical report for your[1] case against the Southern Rayon Company.

Notwithstanding the improvement in your general condition, I[2] have provided a detailed explanation of your injuries and substantiated that you have a permanent[3] disability.

I will be present at the trial and, if questioned, will be prepared to supplement this[4] information with Xrays and case reports. Cordially, (90)

Lesson 8, Page 36

37. Dear Mrs. Washington: It is with exceedingly high hopes and confidence that we announce our furniture and[1] furnishings show, which will be held the last two weeks in March. We are not being immodest in saying that it will[2] be the most successful in Virginia.

We have arranged for specialists in home planning to come from Pittsburgh and[3] New York. Our guests will be invited to confer with them concerning all furnishing problems.

Outstanding values[4] in both domestic and imported articles will be included in the displays. The commerce committee members[5] previewed the plans today and were most encouraging in their opinions.

We are reserving certain afternoons[6] for club groups. Our objective in doing this is to give your members the opportunity to go through the[7] display rooms in comfort. We feel confident you will approve this procedure.

Please write us promptly. After I hear[8] from you, I will be able to send an immediate confirmation. Very cordially yours, (177)

38. To Plant Managers in Houston, Los Angeles, and Portland: It is indeed embarrassing to acknowledge that[1] a competing firm in Vermont has beaten us to the punch on our new eraser. We are not jumping to the[2] conclusion that the situation is hopeless, as we shall have some features now unknown to the competition.[3]

We have acknowledged that the product is as yet unfinished, but we have concluded that it would be disadvantageous[4] to get the eraser on the market immediately. To be impatient now might make it[5] impossible to reach our particular goal later.

We must insist, however, on a careful guarding of all[6] information related to this subject. Furthermore, all employees should be especially reminded of the[7] confidential nature of the new composition used for the eraser. No employee would knowingly give[8] information, of course, but each must be cautioned against any further remarks in this connection. Remind your[9] employees it is to their advantage to avoid any reference to this particular subject. If we[10] are to make this item commercially successful, its special features must be a well-kept company secret.[11]

Please send a strong memo on the subject to everyone in your division. Emphasize the big investment that[12] has gone into this project. And, please be sure to send me a copy as an acknowledgment of the receipt of[13] this memo. C. G. Cummings (265)

39. Dear Jack: A friend who is in service with me in New Mexico injured his forehead while he was on furlough in[1] South Dakota.

He was uneasy about reporting the accident on his return to duty. Since he had[2] no feelings of distress, there seemed no reason to do so.

Recently, his disposition has completely changed.[3] He does not always recognize friends, and he seems emotionally disturbed at times. He refuses to conform. For[4] example, he will not report his comings and goings even when he is on assignment. When questioned, he has[5] forgotten the details, and accuses others of being unfair.

I cannot understand why his behavior[6] has gone unnoticed by everyone but me. While I know he would not forgive me for bringing the matter to your[7] attention, I have complete confidence in your judgment. Please acknowledge immediately and tell me what to[8] do. Martin (162)

40. Dear Mr. Conover: The reports from the Kansas City attorney on the properties you hold there seem to[1] me to be extremely opinionated.

My objection is primarily related to his coverage[2] of the subjects of income and repairs. They might be brought into closer relationship. I cannot understand[3] how he proposes to increase your income so substantially and at the same time allocate so little for[4] maintenance and repairs. J. G. Lorenzo (88)

41. Antonio Rafael: What connotation do you get from the enclosed, unsigned letter?

It states that it would[1] be advantageous to our company to enact a system that would check on the activities—doings, if[2] you please—of our personnel.

The inference, of course, is that some of the people we employ are enriching themselves[3] at company expense.

Do you think we should bring it to the attention of the policies committee? Kevin[4] Connery (83)

Lesson 9, Page 41

42. To All Department Heads: It is particularly gratifying to us to report that yesterday we received[1] word that Thomas Regent, a director of our company, has been appointed to the governor's advisory[2] staff.

This recognition of Mr. Regent's excellent work in serving the public is also a great[3] tribute to his character.

Of course, it is unnecessary to remind those who know him of the effort he[4] has made in developing more progressive personnel policies in this company. These changes have been of[5] unquestioned value as well to those working in similar businesses. J. G. (115)

43. Dear Mr. Defferman: Thank you for your order for a new car. We are wondering whether you would be satisfied[1] with a color other than the one you chose.

Several weeks ago an order was placed for a similar[2] model but the customer now finds that government business is going to take him out of the country. He was[3] not able, therefore, to take the car. His selection was a dark green, while yours was light green.

If you would not object[4] to the substitution, we could make immediate delivery; otherwise, we cannot give you a definite[5] delivery date until the railroad strike is settled.

I hope you will make an appointment to come in as soon[6] as possible to see if you will be satisfied with the different color. We will hold the car for a week,[7] but you will have to let us know by the tenth if you are interested in this suggestion. Cordially yours,[8] (160)

44. Dear Mr. Devlin: In my judgment the luncheon given by the board of governors of the manufacturers[1] association was the most

progressive step that has been taken in many years. I could not help but wish that[2] such a meeting had taken place years ago.

One of the greatest problems faced by most of these businessmen is the[3] lack of adequate transportation facilities, and this was the suggested topic for the meeting that followed.[4]

A railroad official devoted a half-hour to outlining plans for expansion. He suggested the[5] manufacturers define their own future plans and share them with the railroad, reminding them that their own expansion[6] plans would govern what the railroad might or could do to keep up to date with the manufacturers' needs.

A spirit[7] of earnest cooperation characterized the entire meeting and was progressively more evident[8] by the questions that came from the group.

To me, it was unquestionably a most successful meeting. I am[9] sure it is not just wishful thinking to conclude that it will result in great dividends for both the manufacturers[10] and the railroad. I could read into the remarks that I overheard when we were departing that most of[11] us are planning to make every effort to give Mr. Defino the guidance he wants. Cordially yours, (239)

45. Dear Mr. Campo: When I took your order for 20 stoves last week, there was no suggestion of a strike among[1] the workers in the parts plant; but one was called yesterday. We understand negotiations are progressing well;[2] and we hope, and certainly are wishing, for a quick settlement.

I want you to know that once we get into[3] production, it will take about three weeks to get all back orders manufactured. May we, therefore, have your permission[4] to divide your order if we can effect some saving in time by shipping the greater part of your order a[5] few days ahead of the balance? I understood you had several orders for these stoves when you placed your order[6] with us. A partial shipment might make a big difference in meeting the wishes of most of your customers.

If[7] you want us to do this, will you please let us hear from you as soon as you can. Cordially yours, (157)

46. Martin Baxter: It makes little difference who is elected chairman of the sales committee. We have a[1] vital group of executives who, though they may differ in the approach to a problem are working toward the same goal.[2]

With the passage of time, it will be evident that what is victory for one and defeat for another will[3] merely be suggestive of the fact that the real leader, the one who can organize the group and has their loyalty,[4] will be chairman.

I hope you won't read into this that I am not interested in the nominations. I[5] do want to have the opportunity to go over the suggested list—I am sure you have several[6] candidates to propose—and discuss the selection before any names are mentioned. J. C. Devoe (137)

Lesson 10, Page 46

47. Gentlemen: As a result of a defect in the electric wiring recently installed in my home, I[1] have had to turn off the main switch and have been without electricity for several days. Since you submitted[2] an estimate for this electrical work and then a contract, you must admit that it is your responsibility[3] to make the needed repairs as soon as possible.

I have already called you several times about[4] this matter. As I told you, my wife was afraid to use our electric appliances—she wouldn't even use[5] the electric iron — for fear of being electrocuted.

May I hear from you by the end of the week so[6] that it will not be necessary for me to take further action. Very truly yours, (136)

48. Dear John: I am pleased to report that almost all the arrangements for the political rally have been completed.[1] Do you know how many tickets for the outing were sold in ten days? More than one thousand! It is sure to be[2] the most successful rally we have ever had.

We have already had acknowledgments from most of the[3] politically important people in the country. In fact, it is altogether possible that the governor[4] himself will be present.

Everything seems to be working out just fine. We have several speakers lined up, and have[5] also arranged for adult as well as juvenile entertainment.

I expect to be able to submit a[6] list of the food that will be needed in a day or two. A committee is working on the plans, but I do not[7] have a report as yet. Peter (146)

49. Gentlemen: I was in your store this afternoon and placed a c.o.d. order for an electric iron. In[1] tonight's Chronicle I saw an advertisement stating that you are going to offer the same article for[2] practically half price on Thursday.

Naturally, I want to take advantage of the sale, and I plan to do so.[3] Please cancel the c.o.d. order. I will come in Thursday morn-

ing to purchase the iron myself.

I am surprised[4] that the salesgirl did not tell me about this sale. Is it possible she didn't know about it herself? Very[5] truly yours, (102)

50. Dear Mr. Chipley: An article in today's Chronicle pointed up the critical shortage of doctors in[1] this area. I am hopeful that the chamber of commerce will have suggestions to remedy the situation.[2]

For one thing, if we advertised in medical journals as well as newspapers, I believe we might have[3] success in attracting doctors to this area. I am sure there are other ways, too, of doing so.

If everyone[4] on the health committee will meet at my office at 11 a.m. Friday, April 10, I feel sure we[5] would be able to start working toward our ultimate goal. I feel certain that you will all subscribe to any program[6] that seems practical.

Please acknowledge this note, by telephone as soon as you receive it. I am counting on your[7] willingness to attend this special meeting. Cordially yours, (151)

51. Dear Doctor Garcia: We have now completed our plans for the annual conference of the State Medical[1] Association.

Although the agenda speaks for itself, please note that we shall have Dr. George Williams, of Great Britain,[2] a noted electrolysis expert, as our guest speaker on Monday, July 15. Doctor Williams will[3] address us from 10 to 11 a.m., and has invited our membership to prepare outlines of their most[4] difficult cases and submit them to him no later than June 10. Doctor Williams will then address himself to[5] the most interesting problems that we ourselves suggest.

You will want to know, too, that Doctor Williams has set aside[6] 1 to 4 p.m. to consult with members who would like to see him privately. If you will indicate your[7] interest, an appointment will be scheduled.

Equally prominent specialists and surgeons will address us on[8] successive days as indicated on the agenda. For example, Dr. John Kennard, formerly head of the[9] State Medical Board, is the keynote speaker at the banquet Monday night. His successor, Dr. Jason Collins,[10] will address us on Tuesday, July 16, on "The Advantages and Disadvantages of X-ray Therapy."[11]

We are certain that all our members will find it most advantageous to attend these meetings and we hope you[12] can plan to be with us. Cordially yours, (247)

52. Dear Mr. Harrold: Your letter of January 31, requesting transfer of ownership of bonds and[1] which was postmarked February 1, did not reach us until February 6. Unfortunately, you forgot[2] to transmit the bonds with your request, and we wonder whether you have already discovered this oversight.

Perhaps[3] you would find it helpful to have our messenger pick up the bonds, after which we can take care of the transaction[4] and enter the new ownership promptly.

If you will telephone, we shall be glad to make the arrangements. We shall,[5] of course, give the bonded messenger a letter of introduction.

If, on the other hand, you wish to postpone[6] the transfer of ownership until you can come in person, please let us know.

Perhaps you prefer to make transmission[7] via the post office as you originally intended. In that case we urge you to send the bonds by[8] registered mail. Very truly yours, (166)

53. Dear Mr. Paragon: During the recent bad weather we found that the typists and clerks could not gain entrance to[1] their working area on several occasions because the security officer was delayed in reaching[2] the building. Would it interfere with internal security to see that keys are provided for at least one[3] of the supervisors on the office staff?

It would seem necessary to introduce some increase in security[4] personnel in order to include at least one responsible member of the office staff. I shall be[5] glad to arrange interviews with the staff and follow your specifications if this modification of the[6] security program meets with your approval. J. C. Strong (131)

54. Dear Friend: Once again we are asking public support of our annual fund-raising campaign. The purpose of the[1] drive may be familiar to you, but we would like to explain to our new neighbors that the campaign has a dual purpose.[2]

The major portion of the funds is used to perpetuate the annual Fourth of July celebration,[3] a "small town" tradition which, unfortunately, has become less and less a part of the American scene. Any[4] surplus is donated to our Mutual Benefit Fund for disabled firemen and for the families[5] of deceased firemen.

Our program will follow the traditional pattern. The day will begin with a parade[6] and will end with a superb fireworks display.

In between, there will be free rides and contests for the small fry, all[7] carefully supervised. Special events of interest to both young and old are also being planned. The local papers[8] will be furnished with complete details as they are worked out. Watch for them.

To prevent overcrowding, attendance[9] will be limited to township residents and their house guests only. The system that proved so successful in the[10] past will be followed again this year. All adults will have to show an identification tag; children not[11] accompanied by their parents will also be required to display tags. The tags can be obtained from the uniformed[12] fireman who will call at your home for your donation soon after May 31. Or, if you wish, you may[13] mail your contribution in the postpaid envelope. Be sure to include your name and address and the number[14] of tickets required. We shall be very happy to mail them to you. Very truly yours, (297)

55. John Quincy: I want to bring your attention to an outstanding employee—Gerald Cashman—who wishes to be[1] transferred to our New York store. He is a superior employee in every way and is enterprising as[2] well.

Jerry is interested in a transfer because he plans to take courses in interior design and[3] decorating in one of the city colleges. He does not want to interrupt his service with our company,[4] but he is interested in furthering his career.

I am attaching Jerry's personnel records.[5] I am personally much interested in this young man and hope you can act favorably on this request so[6] Jerry can be entered in the college program he has chosen by the fall semester.

I am sure the transfer[7] would help considerably in employee relationships as well. Jerry is extremely popular with the[8] management, as well as with the general staff here, and we would all be pleased if this request could be granted. John Reilly[9] (180)

Lesson 12, Page 57

56. Dear Fred: My niece, Mary Casey, is now bound for New York for the first time. She is looking forward to a brief[1] vacation before starting a new job.

I hope you won't mind, but I did tell her that I would write to see if you could[2] arrange for tickets to two or three of the best shows. If there is a young man in your office who would be willing[3] to escort Mary, the treat is on me. She is an attractive girl with a charming personality. As soon[4] as you let me know the amount to send for the tickets, together with your estimate of any other[5] expenses that may be necessary to make the visit more enjoyable for Mary, I'll mail you my check.[6]

It has been a long time since I have been to New York, but you'll find me dropping in on you one of these days on my way[7] to Washington.

Thanks for anything you do to see that Mary has an unforgettable vacation—and don't[8] be backward in making suggestions. The sky is the limit!

Best wishes to you and Jessie. Sincerely yours,[9] (180)

57. Dear Mr. Gomez: A faculty dinner, honoring our own Dr. Gerald Gray, has been planned for Friday, June[1] 16.

Afterward, Doctor Gray will present one of his stimulating lectures, which he will illustrate with some[2] excellent color slides that he made while visiting the northern countries of Europe.

Reservations must reach our[3] office no later than Friday, May 26. If you want to be sure that there is a place for you, Mr. Gomez,[4] please fill out and return the enclosed card as soon as possible.

We know you won't want to miss the banquet or[5] Doctor Gray's exciting program. Sincerely yours, (109)

58. Gentlemen: This letter is your authority to release to Mr. Gerald Taylor, the bearer, the bonds left[1] in your care on May 1, together with those recently purchased on my telephone order.

You will want to know[2] that I have given power of attorney to Mr. Taylor, and he is acting with that authority.[3]

Mr. Taylor is a boyhood friend, whose loyalty over the years and fine personal qualities, make him worthy[4] of this responsibility. Sincerely yours, (89)

59. Dear Mr. North: At a recent meeting of the Neighborhood Men's Club, the treasurer introduced a resolution[1] to increase dues to $25 a year. Some of the gentlemen now question whether the resolution[2] was acted upon according to proper rules of order.

Apparently there is a dissenting minority,[3] who believe the $5 increase will seriously affect their ability to bring in new members.[4]

We are, therefore, writing to all members reminding them of the next regular meeting—June 10—when the[5] resolution will be presented again. Whether you plan to vote yes or no, please be on hand for the June 10 meeting.[6] Sincerely yours, (124)

60. Dear Mr. Sothern: Do you have the ability to collect overdue payments? In our business we have some[1] accounts that fail to make payment promptly. In this neighborhood type of operation, punctuality of payment[2] is rather important; the majority of our collectors are paid according to the collections they make.[3]

If you have the necessary qualifications and would like to take over two adjacent localities,[4] Mr. Sothern, we shall be glad to make you an attractive offer.

Let us know by an airmail letter or[5] telegram if you are interested, for we are about to list the opening with an agency. We prefer[6] not to make any more contacts, however, until we hear from you. We shall, of course, require information[7] as to your past experience in this type of work, particularly if you were employed in a similar[8] capacity previously. Sincerely yours, (169)

61. Gentlemen: On my last stock order you overlooked two very important items. At least, I suspect you did,[1] because the covering invoice did not indicate that they were on back order; neither did I receive notice[2] that a separate shipment was being made.

I am very much in need of these two items:

25 pint-size,[3] wide-mouth thermos bottles
48 oral thermometers, individually boxed
Please let me know how soon[4] I can count on receiving them. Very truly yours, (90)

Lesson 13, Page 63

62. Dear Mr. Johnston: Circumstances will not permit my undertaking a sales trip to Stamford for another[1] month or two, and I am too selfish to want anyone else to make the trip! If your department managers' meeting[2] can be postponed just a few weeks, I would be more than delighted to participate in your program.

Next week I[3] will be visiting our plants in Harrisburg and Pittsburgh; then I go to Johnstown, Lexington, Nashville, Birmingham,[4] and Jacksonville. I expect to return to the office in about two weeks.

I shall probably use the following[5] two weeks to clear up most of the accumulation of desk work. However, I could be with you the week of[6] May 10—just five weeks from now. I had planned to visit Evanston and Springfield, Illinois, and Davenport, Iowa,[7] first; but I could stop in each of those cities on my way back from California and Washington. I know I[8] sound like an advertisement for an airline with so much jumping around, but you will understand that it cannot be[9] avoided.

Let me know how I can best fit into your program. Which would be the better time—the week of May 10[10] or May 17? It is understood that you have first choice. Very truly yours, (214)

63. Dear Mrs. Oxford: I understand that in a very short time Mr. Oxford is to undergo a serious[1] operation at Morristown Hospital, and I presume this will require a long period of absence[2] from the job.

In order to regulate our work orders until such time as he has made a full recovery,[3] we must undertake the training of another man to assume some of Mr. Oxford's responsibilities[4] temporarily.

You will appreciate that this is a circumstance over which neither he nor we have[5] any control. It is to be understood, however, that Mr. Oxford will retain his job at full salary[6] during the entire period, and on resumption of his regular assignments, his full authority[7] will be reinstated.

We have very much admired Mr. Oxford's self-control during this difficult[8] period of illness and send him our very best wishes for a complete and speedy recovery. Sincerely[9] yours, (181)

64. Dear Mr. Perry: Now that you are up to the $15,000-a-year bracket, are you likely to be[1] self-satisfied and assume that you "have it made"—self-made?

We hope not, though it is safe to speculate that many[2] young men who get to such a position might well be. An equal number, however, are aware of the rapid[3] changes being made in the business world and are preparing to keep abreast of them.

Have you read David Greenfield's[4] *Sales, the Consumer and the Salesman?* Each of the cases presents evidence, circumstantial or factual, that[5] give insight into some new approaches for improving your prospects for bigger and better sales. In an economy[6] like ours, where the rate of consumption of goods is growing by leaps and bounds, the proper sales approach is[7] sure to bring rich rewards to those who know its secret.

Isn't it time you had a copy of David Greenfield's new[8] book? It will give you pointers worth many times its purchase price. Cordially yours, (174)

65. Dear Mr. Grant: I understood that the company would pay the entire cost of my move from Jacksonville to[1] Charleston. I cannot understand why only a portion of the expense has been reimbursed to date.

Did I[2] misunderstand, or was an error in tabulation made so that the amount paid is incorrect? This is my[3] assumption as a result

of the memorandum circulated prior to moving the plant location to[4] Charleston. Also, when, at the company's request I moved from Framingham to Jacksonville, every related expense[5] was reimbursed.

I am sending you a copy of the statement of expenses. If you find it correct under the[6] established policy, I am sure you will want to have a supplementary check issued in the amount[7] of $400, since I have been underpaid that much on the total. For verification, I am again[8] attaching copies of all bills related to the moving costs.

Please help me get this matter cleared up. If[9] I misunderstood what was to be reimbursed, please let me know so that I can take care of the matter myself.[10] Cordially yours, (203)

Lesson 14, Page 67

66. Mr. Rivera: Last week our president, Mr. Lake, advocated a change in our company's insurance[1] program. Before inaugurating a new program, however, he would like to investigate all the types of[2] insurance available to make sure that we get the best possible program.

You have an excellent insurance[3] background; consequently, Mr. Lake has asked that the job of studying various institutional insurance[4] programs be assigned to you. As you know, a number of studies have been made during the past two years; to avoid[5] duplication, you may want to look over the figures that have already been gathered. I will see if I[6] can locate some of this material here and send it to you today.

Could you give this matter your attention[7] during the next month? It seems to me that your best contribution can be made by checking into what is available[8] to see which plan is most adequate for our requirements and the cost of instituting the plan.

Mr.[9] Lake has asked me to express his gratitude for your help. After you are through with your study, he will no doubt[10] thank you in person. By the way, how do you like your new location? Jerry Casey (215)

67. Dear Mrs. Nestor: I am sorry that I cannot excuse your son Jimmy on the basis of the explanation[1] offered for his absence from classes last Tuesday.

There were a number of absences on the day in question,[2] and an inquiry at the local theater indicates that your son, along with several other boys, spent the[3] day there. Surely, therefore, his absence could not be attributed to tonsillitis, as the excuse indicates.[4]

Aptitude tests indicate that Jimmy could be an outstanding student, but despite this aptitude his frequent[5] absences and his attitude are preventing him from meeting the requirements of a number of his courses.[6]

I hope you will cooperate by making certain that any subsequent absences on Jimmy's part are[7] accompanied by valid excuses. Very truly yours, (150)

68. Dear Doctor Fisher: I must apologize for the delay in sending you a check for the neuritis treatments[1] that I received last month. I returned today from a trip to Atlantic City and other parts of the state and[2] found your reminder waiting for me.

I am feeling quite well now. Before I received the treatments, the pains almost[3] drove me frantic; lately, however, I have had no pain whatsoever. I attribute this improvement to the[4] excellent way in which you handled my case. Cordially yours, (91)

69. Dear Mrs. Conant: We are very glad to have you inquire again about the oil painting offered in[1] a private sale by the Atlantic Art Society. When you initially inquired, we assumed you were[2] an art dealer or distributor, to whom the sale is closed. Please accept our apology.

It is an authentic[3] Whistler, as can be verified by the date and the distinguishable signature. Originally owned by[4] a Belgian family, it was confiscated during World War II. Their proprietary right has since been affirmed.[5]

Because the present owner is in need of funds, the painting was brought here, and the Atlantic Art Society[6] has the authority to take over the closed bid sale. If a reasonable offer is among those[7] submitted, it will not be refused. If two offers in the same amount are received, a bid-off will be instituted[8] between the parties, and the highest bid shall effect a sale. Cordially yours, (174)

70. Dear Dean Edens: I am inquiring about the psychology courses offered at State. What constitutes the[1] prerequisites? How many days each week does the advanced psychology class meet and at what hours? Are the[2] instructors practicing psychologists?

I have taken a number of courses in related subject areas.[3] Will my transcript be adequate for admission? Cordially yours, (72)

71. Dear Miss Brady: Your contribution to the Constitutional Society is greatly appreciated.[1]

We are also in need of volunteer workers. Would you contribute some time as well? We need ten or more people[2] to distribute pamphlets at meetings to be held within the next month.

We frequently need help in handling[3] inquiries at headquarters.

One requirement is that anyone unable to fulfill a scheduled[4] assignment, is expected to arrange substitute coverage.

You will, we know, enjoy the fellowship of serving[5] with the people who have contributed so much to this cause. Cordially yours, (114)

Lesson 15, Page 72

72. Dear Mrs. Held: Your mailman will soon bring you a recent issue of *World Travel*. We hope that through this magazine[1] you will enjoy a tour of the English countryside and visits to the historic castles of England. In[2] addition to the "tour," there is a capsule history of Great Britain in full color.

Future issues will cover[3] Hawaii and other islands of the South Pacific, Canada, Puerto Rico, and the mainland of the[4] U.S.A., to mention just a few of the interesting places you can visit right at home.

We should like to[5] have you take advantage of a significant saving by accepting the anniversary subscription rates[6] offered on the convenient order form enclosed. Cordially yours, (132)

73. Memo to Executive Personnel: In the past it has been our custom to permit some of our people to[1] take their vacation in days. It is now necessary that we establish a new policy that requires[2] all vacations be taken in one-week units because of the problems created for the payroll department[3] where exceptions are made.

Will you please see that everyone reporting to you schedules vacations for a week[4] or two at a time.

Also, it is important that each department prepare a vacation schedule, listing[5] employees in alphabetical order, and file a copy with payroll. This request has special significance,[6] since failure to comply may cause inconvenience to those who do not get vacation pay in advance.

One or[7] two exceptions may develop in the course of the business year. These, however, must be kept to a minimum,[8] and the privilege should be extended only when it will be a convenience to the company.

The executive[9] committee in special meeting has authorized this preliminary announcement and suggests that you call[10] it to the attention of your staff immediately. This means, of course, that you should let anyone out of the[11] office know by mail as soon as possible. L. M. Fernandez (232)

74. To the Faculty: More and more schools are adopting the new arithmetic and, to keep up to date, our school board[1] has recommended that it be included in our three township schools.

A special course is being offered by one[2] of our own staff members, who has a certificate from American University. Full credit will, therefore,[3] be given to all who complete the course.

We should like to have all teachers of Grades 1 through 4 in the first session,[4] teachers of Grades 5 through 8 in the second session. The first group will meet September 1 and 2; group two,[5] September 3 and 4.

If you will be out of town, or if for any reason the dates scheduled are inconvenient,[6] you will want to know that a second evening seminar is being scheduled immediately following[7] school opening. Dates and hours will be announced shortly.

Please indicate on the appropriate line[8] in which seminar you wish to take part. If you are unable to participate in the pre-school opening[9] seminar, please be sure that you do not plan any after-school appointments during the week of September 14.[10]

If you completed an equivalent course during the summer, you will, of course, be excused. We should be reluctant[11] to excuse anyone, however, without evidence of satisfactory completion of the course. (238)

75. Inventory and Sales Personnel: A new tax law, based on inventories, has just been passed. It is essential[1] that as of March 30 our reserve stock be at the lowest possible point to reduce the tax payment[2] to the minimum.

For the present, we would suggest that you estimate the stock that will be required through that date;[3] then, except where prices of new stock may vary considerably, place all stock replenishment orders for[4] delivery on May 1 or later.

Wherever possible, avoid putting into stock any items that could[5] be held over and that will not be used until fall. Some of these would be merchandise for Christmas sale.

By the way,[6] some of you have written to ask if American flags and the books *See America First* and *U.S. History*[7] are tax exempt. That information is given in a separate memorandum that is attached. Carlos[8] Gonzales (160)

Lesson 16, Page 78

76. Dear Mrs. Ramos: We are pleased to send you the schedule of performances to be offered by the Little[1] Theater during its summer season. We are proud to announce that, in addition to several Shakespearian[2] productions, we shall give some of the Victor Herbert operettas.

It is your special privilege as a charter[3] member, to be in the first group to select dates. Your quota is one pair of tickets for each performance. We[4] are holding the best seat locations until the week of April 1 for you. Kindly circle the dates of your choice,[5] and return the form as quickly as possible.

During April and May, we shall be presenting a revival[6] of *The Winter's Tale* for our annual school program. You will be given an opportunity to see this play[7] on selected evenings at a discount of $2 a seat, as specified on the special order form[8] attached. If you wish to take advantage of these discount prices, indicate the date and the number of seats you[9] want and enclose your check for the total amount. Very truly yours, (193)

77. To the Members of the Violin Club: Prior to the social meeting on Tuesday evening, March 15, there[1] will be a very brief business meeting—just 20 minutes. The subject is listed on the enclosed agenda.[2]

To review the previous announcement about this meeting: Miss Julia Owens is going to play the violin[3] and Edwin Philips, the viola. They will be accompanied by Marian Law at the piano. An[4] interesting treat is in store for all of us.

Some of you have asked when the meeting will break up. You should be able[5] to get away any time after 9:30. Those wishing to stay beyond that time, however, may make use[6] of the radio or the television.

Watch this board for an announcement that will be posted on March 20.[7]

The March 15 meeting will begin at 7:10 instead of 7:30; please do plan to come. (157)

78. Miss Freeman: Would any of the employees in your division be interested in overtime work for[1] approximately a three-month period? If so, I would appreciate your advising me because we are looking[2] for additional help in the billing department for the months of November through January.

Those[3] interested should be told that they will be expected to report for work twice each week from six to eight. The hourly[4] wage for this job is $2.75.

One young man from your division, a William Twining, came[5] to us this week requesting extra work. What can you tell me about him? While we liked him, we told him we would prefer[6] that he work through you; therefore, we did not say "yes."

Please be sure to let me know about those

people on your staff[7] whom you would recommend and who might be interested in this opportunity for extra income.

I'm in[8] rather a hurry, so I hope you will be able to forward the names of two or three prospects to me soon. J.[9] G. Devlin (182)

79. Dear Mr. Powers: The board of directors has approved your recommendation to extend an invitation[1] to buyers and assistant buyers to attend a special showing of the new materials that will be used[2] in our dress and suit line this fall. They have asked that you include members of the Fashion Bureau in your invitation.[3]

They have requested that you write an announcement that will create general interest in the fall line.

Before[4] you go ahead on your own with further plans, please come to my office and let's discuss the details outlined above.[5] We will not submit any further plans until we feel quite certain they will be received and approved without question.[6] We don't want to have to do any last-minute switching. Fred Kerr P.S. Watch for a package of fabrics, sent[7] from Italy, which you should receive soon. (147)

Lesson 17, Page 83

80. Dear Mr. Johnson: I wish I could describe our life insurance program to your management team and tell them of[1] the opportunities afforded by group membership. Although our plan is not offered to the general public,[2] it is under federal jurisdiction.

Won't you look over the description of the plan in the enclosed[3] booklet and then discuss the rates with some of your top men? If you would like to have extra copies of the booklet,[4] please give me the names of the persons to whom they should be addressed and the number I should supply. Of course, the copies[5] are free; you will receive your shipment within two weeks after we hear from you.

In that connection, may I[6] have your permission to say you submitted the names?

Other firms in this area that are participating[7] in our plan are listed in the booklet. Experience proves that employees appreciate the reduced rates and the[8] increased benefits that membership in our plan offers them.

Employee payments, of course, are by means of monthly[9] payroll deductions. Payment to us would follow your receipt of an invoice for the total premium.

Please use[10] the enclosed reply card or telephone me so that I may explain further the substantial benefits your[11] employees will receive through the protection our plan provides. Cordially yours, (232)

81. Dear Miss Carter: As you may recall, our committee is to meet again on May 15 to make the decision[1] as to those who ultimately will be granted loans and the amount of each loan.

Perhaps you have students who[2] qualify under the regulations outlined in the printed form attached. Encourage them to complete the application[3] and submit it to the loan committee without delay. Cordially, (74)

82. Dear Mr. Conroy: Unfortunately, it is impossible for me to meet you at the airport on Monday,[1] March 6, as I must begin jury duty that morning. Frank Cummings will be there in my place.

As you already[2] know, I was to submit my report on Purchasing Furniture and Equipment. Perhaps you would be willing to[3] give it for me. My secretary is keeping a copy of the report for you at my office and is also[4] sending one in another mail so that you will have time to look it over before March 6.

You will notice[5] the report includes some unfinished business from our January meeting. I was asked to comment especially[6] on some of the items that were tabled temporarily. I am opposed to statements four and six and feel[7] they should not be enacted, because we have not been furnished with enough information. I have explained my[8] reasons in detail in the report.

I am extremely sorry that this jury duty came up, as I wanted so[9] much to see you. I am almost certain a mistake has been made, as I was foreman of a jury just recently.[10] Perhaps they will decide to dismiss or reject me. At any rate, I hope I am going to see you before[11] you must return to Cleveland's suburbs. Sincerely yours, P.S. While you are here, make it a point to see our new[12] library—everyone has been impressed. (247)

83. The Competent Secretary Saves the Employer's Time

Let us examine the procedures of at least three competent secretaries.

One saves time for her employer[1] by writing letters "on approval" that come in for her employer to answer. She gathers the facts pertaining[2] to the question at hand and then drafts a reply just as she believes her employer would write it.

This same[3] secretary saves time for her employer, too, by knowing when to ask questions. It is no disgrace to ask questions,[4] although some secretaries seem to think so. This secretary knows when she knows, but she also knows when she doesn't.[5]

Another secretary saves time by her tactful handling of many people who visit the office each day.[6] Her employer said, "My secretary is able to talk with people and turns over to me only those who[7] need my special attention."

Our third employer sang the praises of his secretary by saying, "She always[8] puts work on my desk that I can sign without correction. She knows that every time something has to be given back[9] to her, it is a waste of my time as well as hers—in other words, that spells 'inefficiency.' "

While the employers[10] of these three secretaries emphasized the saving of time, each made one other comment that is worth noting:[11]

She does not get emotionally disturbed if I must return work.

She is always immaculately groomed.

She[12] is forever performing tasks beyond the call of duty. (250)

Lesson 18, Page 88

84. Dear Member: Our annual meeting is scheduled for Thursday night, June 14.

Mr. S. C. Long, director[1] of the Pittsburgh Hospital (formerly with the Princeton Hospital in Newburgh), will give a brief lecture on[2] hospital record keeping and accounting efficiency as practiced in his institution. We believe this[3] presentation will be extremely beneficial to all of us.

Also, we have scheduled an important film[4] entitled "Efficient Hospital Operation and the Effect on Patients," narrated by Dr. John Stamford, which[5] will be especially helpful to those who have recently entered the field.

Don't bother to write, just come! Sincerely,[6] (121)

85. Dear Miss Strong: You will be glad to learn that after checking further we were able to approve payments for your[1] hospital care following your recent operation. Actually, payment would have been approved more readily,[2] if your most recent hospitalization card had been presented on admission.

In the future, please use the[3] one with the contract number shown above. This is the only official and acceptable card at present.[4] We recommend that you dispose of any that were issued earlier. Retaining them will only create[5] confusion should you present one of them on another occasion.

Note that the contract number includes both the group[6] and your individual number. If you don't have a card bearing the above number, you may easily[7] obtain one by contacting the personnel department of the Plainfield and Hartford Press—the group under which you are[8] currently enrolled.

If you have already sent a check in payment, a proper adjustment, together with receipts,[9] will come directly from the hospital. We are glad to have been of assistance. Cordially, Admissions[10] Department (202)

86. Dear Mr. Orlando: Welcome to the growing list of satisfied customers who say, "Charge it, please" at one of[1] Nashville's outstanding stores—National Department Store.

Your application was processed quickly, Mr. Orlando,[2] because of your excellent credit record. Therefore, your account is ready for use when you visit our great store.[3] Our entire staff will do everything possible to make your shopping pleasant and satisfying.

You will receive[4] a monthly statement of purchases made shortly after our closing date for billings—the 20th of each[5] month. If your account is paid within 30 days after receipt of our statement, no service charge is ever made.

Enjoy[6] your charge account to the fullest by taking advantage of the many special services we offer:[7] telephone shopping, free parking (less than a block away on Water Street), prompt and efficient delivery throughout[8] the city and suburbs, and gift wrapping.

Come in often to shop or just to make yourself "at home" as you browse. You[9] are always welcome at the National Department Store. Sincerely yours, (193)

87. Dear Mr. Adams: The chances are 15 to 1 that you're working extremely hard. By "working extremely hard,"[1] I mean working under great daily pressure, with needless effort for the net results that you attain.

How can I[2] make that statement? For over seventy-five years my company has studied the work methods of thousands of[3] business and professional people like you. Many set too high a pace for themselves, only to have fatigue set in[4] long before it should. We've been able to show 14 out of 15 of them (myself included) a pleasant short[5] cut to accomplishment.

We have prepared a 12-page booklet called *Making More Time*. It is an idea-packed, step-by-step[6] analysis of modern executive work methods. It shows how busy men can get more work done with much[7] less effort. It is an eye-opening booklet, full of helpful ideas for simplifying your job.

We are going[8] to assume you will be eager to get a copy, so we are reserving one for you. Just initial and[9] return this letter in the enclosed envelope. Cordially, (191)

88. Gentlemen: Did our national advertising campaign result in another spurt of orders for you? We are[1] now ready to introduce local promotion that has managed to set a great record in the northern and western[2] parts of the country, in particular.

Please keep careful sales records over a period of three months on[3] this merchandise. This information will be useful in verifying the effectiveness of these two types of[4] sales promotion and helpful in working out desirable changes that would result in even better sales next year.[5]

We feel it no presumption on our part to say, "We are confident you will find that sales of our products will[6] be better than ever." Very truly yours, (128)

Lesson 19, Page 93

89. Dear Mr. Cunningham: You had justification in writing to ask about the introductory technical[1] training course. It will be offered in about three weeks, and there will be three meetings a week. We have had to[2] postpone the class because several members of our faculty have been ill. Our failure to issue any[3] notification about the opening of the class wasn't an oversight.

It will be worth waiting for. We know you will[4] like the program offerings and will be pleased with our excellent instructors—all students have been.

Your name is[5] entered in our records to receive information as soon as the final date is settled. Cordially yours, (119)

90. Dear Mrs. Wellington: Circumstances have so improved that our organization is going to be able[1] to entertain the young people at the hospital. A program that should be of interest to all the youngsters[2] has been arranged.

I am chairman for the entertainment section and have been asked to tell you that when our supervisor[3] first visited your young people, she circulated a questionnaire which each youngster filled out, telling what[4] he would like to see and do. Since then, a tabulation has been made. It is self-evident that a circus type[5] of "show" is what they most want.

The accumulation of data indicates you have some superior and[6] enterprising young people, as a number offered to help with the program. Their cooperation was outstanding,[7] Mrs. Wellington.

We don't want to overlook the slightest talent, so we thought we would have an audition to[8] better channel their abilities. However, before we do, we would be grateful if you will answer the questions[9] on the enclosed postcard. It is necessary, too, that I visit your hospital to check the electrical[10] outlets, the facilities for refreshments, and some other details.

I plan to be in your neighborhood on[11] the fifth. Would that be a convenient day for you to see me? Please telephone to let me know. Sincerely, (239)

91. Dear Bob: This is by way of an introduction to Mr. James Framingham. I asked him to call to see you soon.[1] I think he would be an effective sales person for you.

I met Mr. Framingham about four years ago.[2] He was still in college then, but had accepted a job as a trainee with one of the life insurance companies.[3] Even then I was impressed with him, and I have seen a lot of him since.

I don't feel you knowingly have been slighting[4] me, Bob, but how about having lunch with me some day soon? Afterward, I can tell you more about Jim Framingham.[5] Sincerely, (102)

92. Mr. Perez: Congratulations on the superb idea you introduced by way of the suggestion box! You[1] showed great familiarity with the subject; therefore, we are asking you to come before our International[2] Committee to demonstrate what you have transferred to paper.

You have full authority to make your presentation[3] in any way you wish. We shall not interfere; neither shall we permit interruption. Instead, discussion[4] on anything not fully understood will be postponed until the demonstration has been completed.

It[5] must have taken considerable time to translate all those technical terms into simple language that the layman[6] can understand. We thank you for your unselfishness.

I have been wondering if our electric wiring[7] will be adequate. Please phone me at Extension 372, to set a time for you to look over the room[8] to be used for the presentation.

If there is something I can do to help before you introduce your material,[9] let me know. James Carson (186)

93. Dear Mr. Murdock: One of the direct benefits of membership in the Managers Guild is our monthly[1] bulletin. In the next issue, for instance, we are having a report on government salaries for clerical[2] employees. You will find much valuable and factual information that will be useful as a basis[3] for revising your own salary standards. Another article of even more pertinent interest is entitled[4] "How to Ask For and Get Cooperation That

Will Increase Production."

We are extending an invitation[5] to you to join our association. You will find membership in the Guild will be helpful in taking over[6] the responsibilities of your new position.

Why not reply immediately and plan to join us[7] for our monthly luncheon in the Convention Room of the Market Street Hotel the first Monday of next month. Cordially,[8] (160)

Lesson 20, Page 98

94. Secretarial Attributes

A business executive was telling a group of secretarial students, soon to be graduated, about[1] the best secretary he ever had.

"Above all, she created goodwill. She had cultivated a good[2] memory. She could remember all our regular customers, and it made them feel important to be greeted[3] by name when they telephoned me or walked into my office.

"She took care of my appointment book and checked up on me[4] in a tactful way if my work fell behind schedule. She knew when I could be interrupted and when not. She used[5] good judgment and wasn't afraid to take a chance. Neither did she think it reduced her status to sharpen my pencils[6] and dust my desk."

The better-than-average secretary doesn't just happen. She is well trained. A beginner[7] does not often start as a secretary. If she has had good training and has confidence in herself and her[8] ability, she should be willing to work as a stenographer until she has her feet on the ground. Then after[9] she has acquired experience and a certain amount of poise, she will be ready to fill that much-envied[10] post of secretary. (204)

95. Dear Mrs. Gentry: You will soon receive a box containing a small personal gift. It is my "thank you" for a[1] wonderful visit.

You divided your time in such a way that no one was ever neglected. In addition,[2] I noticed you had a wonderful system that immediately put all your guests at ease. We liked that family[3] feeling, but many of us felt we could never attempt to accomplish what you did. The entire group commented,[4] too, on the spirit of friendly competition that prevailed during the playing of the games. No wonder your[5] friends are so devoted to you!

Once more, thanks for one of the best week's vacation I ever had. Fondly, (117)

96. Dear Neighbor: You no doubt have heard the news of the persistent effort to place a giant jetport, the largest in[1] the world,

in your neighborhood. A permanent committee of local residents, whose names are listed on this[2] letterhead, has been formed to express opposition to this serious proposal—it will try to prevent it.

We[3] definitely believe that it would bring about chaos in our fine residential town. We could no longer maintain[4] our pleasant suburban way of life.

Funds are urgently needed to carry on a really effective program[5] of opposition. Surely you will send a contribution to help us continue our efforts to prevent[6] the proposed jetport.

We meet the first Monday of the month at 8 p.m. in the Civic Center. We'd like you to[7] come to our meetings to examine the various reports we have on display. Very sincerely, (158)

97. Dear Alumnus: The School of Business Administration and Commerce will hold its annual meeting in Room[1] 55 of Alumni Hall on Saturday, June 17, at 10 a.m.

A luncheon will follow the meeting[2] promptly. It will be held in the large cafeteria adjacent to the Administration and Commerce Building.[3]

We would like to reserve a place for you at the luncheon. (There are three price ranges, with a minimum of $3.)[4] All that is necessary is to sign and return the enclosed sheet.

If you cannot make the luncheon, you might[5] wish to send a donation—it can be mailed today. I am sure you know that donations and money from the luncheon[6] help to cover the education costs of deserving students.

Do come and join us at this important event.[7] Cordially, (143)

98. Dear Mrs. Bennett: We are concerned about the fact that your charge account has not been used recently. If there has[1] been a change in your name or address, or if we have been at fault in any way, don't fail to call it to our[2] attention.

This spring our four stores, listed at the top of this letter, have their usual complete and modern assortments[3] of stunning fashions, smart accessories, and gifts for every member of the family at our usual low[4] sale prices.

Every member of our organization looks forward to serving you from month to month. Why don't you[5] return the enclosed card and continue to shop in our friendly stores. Very truly yours, (116)

99. Dear Mr. Powers: As you know, I am to deliver a paper on stocks and bonds before an estimated[1] audience of 75 at your company on Thursday night, February 17.

Mr. Frank[2] Cummings, a representative of Harding and Rushmore, will be my assistant at my demonstration. I feel,[3] however, that I should be assistant to Mr. Cummings, as he represents one of the most outstanding firms in[4] the country in the field of investment services. I must mention the credit that is due Mr. Cummings, as[5] he edited my paper.

My reason for writing so early is to ask whether you believe there will be a[6] demand for booklets regarding our subject.

A brief statement on the bottom of this letter is sufficient, Mr.[7] Powers. Cordially yours, (145)

Key to Chart on Inside Back Cover

Brief Forms of Gregg Shorthand in Alphabetical Order

1. A-an, about, acknowledge, advantage, advertise, after.
2. Am, and, are-our-hour, at-it, be-by, between,
3. Big, business, but, can, character, circular.
4. Company, correspondence, could, difficult, during, enclose.
5. Envelope, ever-every, experience, for, from, general.
6. Gentlemen, glad, gone, good, govern, great.
7. Have, his-is, how-out, I, Idea, immediate.
8. Importance-important, in-not, manufacture, merchandise, merchant, morning.
9. Mr., Mrs., must, never, newspaper, next.
10. Object, of, one-won, opinion, opportunity, order.
11. Ordinary, organize, over, part, particular, present.
12. Probable, progress, public, publication-publish, purpose, put.
13. Quantity, question, railroad, recognize, regard, regular.
14. Request, responsible, satisfactory-satisfy, send, several, shall.
15. Short, should, situation, soon, speak, state.
16. Street, subject, success, such, suggest, than.
17. Thank, that, the, their-there, them, they.
18. Thing-think, this, those, throughout, time, under.
19. Upon, use, value, very, was, well-will.
20. Were-year, what, when, where, which, why.
21. Wish, with, work, world, worth, would.
22. Yesterday, yet, you-your.